"It is my honor and privilege to endorse Mary Jo Sharp and her book, *Defending the Faith: Apologetics in Women's Ministry*. In this book, Mary Jo calls the women leaders in ministry to take their place in apologetics. Way to go, Mary Jo! After reading this book all women will understand more clearly our call to equip and encourage the women we influence to understand not only what we believe, but to then represent our beliefs in a concise and convincing method. Mary Jo makes her case of convincing every woman to defend Christianity.

After reading this book you will be challenged to go deeper in your study of why we believe what we do as Christians. Mary Jo presents a convincing case with passion, conviction, and humor. You will know Mary Jo when you finish this book. I am so proud to call Mary Jo my friend and colaborer in the faith."

—Pam Brewer,
Director of Women to Women Ministry,
First Baptist, Dallas, Texas

"*Defending the Faith* is a ground-breaking book for women. I hope and pray it will help inspire many women to learn how to defend their faith so they can have an impact on both their families and the wider culture. I will be giving a copy to my wife as well as the rest of her small group as soon as it's available!"

—Sean McDowell, speaker, educator, and author,
Apologetics for a New Generation

"Mary Jo Sharp is not only one of America's foremost female apologists, she's one of our foremost apologists, period. This book is a call for churches to be serious about discipling the mind of its women, and it couldn't come at a better time for me. I'm glad my three daughters will grow up having this resource in their hands and can know the opportunity and calling they have to courageously defend truth in their words and their lives."

—John Stonestreet, speaker and fellow,
The Chuck Colson Center for Christian Worldview

"Mary Jo Sharp is uniquely qualified to equip Christian women to always be ready to give a defense for what they believe. Her passion for truth, for articulating it in a well-reasoned and attractive way, and for sharing it with those who desperately need Christ is a model that is on full display in this book. *Defending the Faith: Apologetics in Women's Ministry* is sure to be the blueprint on how to encourage apologetics in women's ministry."

—Doug Powell, author/designer,
Resurrection iWitness and *Jesus iWitness*

"Mary Jo Sharp has written a book that was needed decades ago. She has filled the need with wit, candor, and intellectual acumen. Professor Sharp has practical experience talking to women all over the country and in an academic community. She is the one of the best communicators in apologetics today, and this book is an example of those skills. Men need to read this book as well as women because it disabuses several foolish beliefs some men might have. At the same time, Professor Sharp affirms the traditional Christian faith."

—John Mark N. Reynolds,
Provost and Professor of Philosophy,
Houston Baptist University

"Drawing on Scripture, the work of Christian scholars, and a wide range of personal experience, Mary Jo Sharp has delivered a strong apologia for building apologetics into women's ministry. My wife, Sharon, and I read this thoughtful, arresting work together—and hope that will many will take up both this book and its cause."

—Mark Coppenger,
Professor of Christian Apologetics,
Southern Baptist Theological Seminary

"Too often we have been comfortable with 'what my parents/church/Sunday school teacher told us' without personally investigating *why* we believe what we believe regarding our faith in Christ. I am thrilled Mary Jo has found a way to not only defend her faith in the daily walk of life, but also to teach others how to do it. Thank you, Mary Jo."

—Chris Adams,
Women's Ministry Specialist, Speaker, and Leadership Trainer

"*Defending the Faith: Apologetics in Women's Ministry* is a must book for those women who are in leadership desiring to have a greater impact on all generations, as well as those women who long to understand how to define their faith. I have seen firsthand how the women across the state of Texas were drawn to a unique way of teaching God's word by Mary Jo Sharp that was helping them answer the reason and evidences for our Christian hope. This woman is a gifted writer and teacher and can take the most complex questions and doubts we face and teach them in such a way that is clear and memorable. Mary Jo will surely leave a legacy as a woman who defended her faith."

—Shirley Moses, author of *Heart Friends*,
Founder of Beyond the Call Ministries

"Mary Jo Sharp has a remarkable ability to make high-level Christian thinking in theology, philosophy, and apologetics accessible to everyone. Her new book, *Defending the Faith*, adds another dimension as well—it connects with women in the church like nothing I've ever seen. This book is personal, engaging, smart, and simply delightful to read. I could not encourage church leaders more to get everyone in the congregation reading this book. Serious spiritual growth in mind and character is certain to occur!"

—Craig J. Hazen,
Founder and Director of the Christian Apologetics program,
Biola University

"Finally, a book that focuses on the use of Christian apologetics in women's ministry! Women's ministry is a powerful element in churches; it meets needs and changes lives for the better. And there has been a recent surge of interest in women's ministry for Christian apologetics. Therefore, this book is both timely and right on the mark, and Mary Jo Sharp is the woman most qualified to teach on the matter. So whether you're a leader or attendee in the church, if you're involved in women's ministry, this is a book you will want to read."

—Michael R. Licona,
Associate Professor in Theology,
Houston Baptist University

"In a unique volume, Mary Jo Sharp has done what very few other scholars could do: challenge women to know more about the contents of their faith and, in particular, how to defend it. A very popular conference speaker and a trained apologist, Sharp reaches out to women, encouraging them to consciously join the ranks of those who are able to provide answers to anyone who wonders how Christianity can be grounded, and doing so with intellectual rigor. With their family members, friends, coworkers, churches, and others, women have matchless opportunities to reach others. This book provides many resources, including how to begin immediately and how to apply apologetics in the context of women's ministry. Thanks to Kregel Publications, too, for providing a distinctive volume that fills such a necessary and neglected area."

—Gary R. Habermas,
Distinguished Research Professor,
Liberty University & Theological Seminary

"What a valuable resource! We live in a culture of competing ideas and ideologies that challenge our faith and require us to think deeply about our beliefs. Honestly, I can't think of a more valuable resource in women's ministry to equip you, your family, and your church to defend your hope in Jesus Christ."

—Andy Steiger,
Director of Apologetics Canada

"Mary Jo Sharp advocates opening a vast new front in the battle for truth by challenging women's ministries to take apologetics training seriously. It's an outstanding idea. Women as a group have always been a critical part of the church's witness, whether through evangelism or civilization-sustaining good deeds. If congregations take *Defending the Faith* seriously, it could equip a whole new generation to love God with their minds."

— Jeff Myers,
President,
Summit Ministries

Apologetics in
Women's Ministry

DE FEND ING THE FAITH

MARY JO SHARP

Kregel
Ministry

Defending the Faith: Apologetics in Women's Ministry

© 2012 by Mary Jo Sharp.

Published by Kregel Publications, a division of Kregel, Inc., P.O. Box 2607, Grand Rapids, MI 49501.

The Greek font GraecaU is available from www.linguistsoftware.com/lgku.htm, +1-425-775-1130.

Library of Congress Cataloging-in-Publication Data
Sharp, Mary Jo, 1974-
    Defending the faith : apologetics in women's ministry / Mary Jo Sharp.
        p. cm.
1. Apologetics. 2. Church work with women. 3. Women in church work. I. Title.
    BT1103.S53 2012
    239.082—dc23

2012034509

ISBN 978-0-8254-3872-1

Printed in the United States of America
16 / 5 4 3 2

For the Christian women of Texas,
who greatly encouraged
the writing of this book.

For Marie,
an inspiring woman
who is more spirited than lions.

And for Roger & Emily,
sojourners in the search for truth
and advocates of good cheer!

Contents

INTRODUCTION

"Jo, you ought to be a lawyer." I cannot recall exactly when my father jokingly expressed this sentiment, but I seem to remember it from junior high. He was referring not only to my inclination to argue with him but also to my strong-willed, perfectionist nature. When particularly annoyed with me, my mom would jest, "Insanity is hereditary: you get it from your children." Looking back, I see no good reason why my parents are still sane after having raised their three children, especially given my countless arguments and debates with them over pretty much everything. I would tell my parents, "I don't mind doing what you ask me, if you'd just give me a reason why," but in reality, even that wouldn't be enough. I would challenge their reasons, debating with them about whether or not they were acceptable. I loved to learn, to question, and to argue. I still do. I am a skeptic, questioning of most everything that comes my way. Dad says that I was born arguing.

My background affects the goal of this book, in which I am, essentially, arguing that Christian women need to be able to defend their faith with intellectual rigor and honesty. I am a believer in God, but I was not raised in an evangelical home or church, and I still feel somewhat like a bull in a china shop whenever I'm involved in evangelical women's ministry. The first time I spoke at my home church was at the annual ladies' tea. My presentations were less refined back then, and as I expounded upon argument after argument for God's existence, I felt like I was smashing my way through the beautifully displayed china. So I ask for grace where I tend to be rough around the edges.

However, in speaking to women's groups around the country, I have found an increasing number of women who are excited to stand for the truth about God. This is where my skeptical attitude deeply connects me to the women of the church: in searching for answers. Women want answers for the questions about faith they receive from coworkers, friends, family, their children, and from their own doubts. And they want to be able to communicate those answers in spite of feeling clumsy or somewhat embarrassed for not understanding a few finer points along the way. It isn't necessary to obtain a formal degree but it is necessary to carefully examine one's beliefs and their foundations.

Early twentieth-century Christian pastor and author A. W. Tozer was never formally trained in theology, yet he expressed the importance of study and examination of belief in God: "Our real idea of God may lie buried under the rubbish of conventional religious notions and may require an intelligent and vigorous search before it is finally unearthed and exposed for what it is. Only after an ordeal of painful self-probing are we likely to discover what we actually believe about God."[1] In our search for answers to the tough questions, we must also be intellectually honest with our own beliefs. Have you ever taken the time to think through exactly what it is you believe about God? Have you thought about *why* you believe in God? If the foundation for belief is untrustworthy, then the whole structure laid upon that foundation is apt to crumble. A solid foundation in God requires your own raw inquiry into faith. You must challenge yourself to provide reasons for your convictions. Many of the people I encounter who left their faith never did this sort of examination until they had been badly hurt by someone in the church or suffered greatly through a painful experience. By that point, people are frequently looking for a reason to leave, not necessarily for brutally honest answers.

I fear that many evangelical women have so much going on in their lives that they do not attend to even the most basic questions about their own beliefs. When a woman does not have a solid basis for belief, she tends to live as a practical atheist. One of the questions

---

1. A. W. Tozer, *The Knowledge of the Holy* (New York: Harper Collins, 1992), 3.

I am asked most frequently is, "How do you explain the hypocrisy of believers?" In other words, why are those who assent to the truth of God's existence and assert the power of God to change lives not actually living as if this claim is true? Certainly, it's a valid question which is probably familiar to many of us. Though I usually respond with an answer encompassing the problem of humankind's fallen nature and the need for Jesus' solution, there is another aspect to consider. Our actions flow from what we *really* believe. Thus, if a woman hasn't deeply examined her current beliefs and compared them to what the Bible has to say, it is possible for her to act contrary to the Christian ethic. If she hasn't probed her own doubts and addressed them adequately, her faith and thereby her actions will make that clear. An uncertain, shaky faith in God will not result in a life of power, boldness, love, and self-control such as Paul described in 2 Timothy 1:7. How do we get there? The apostle Peter instructs Christians to honor Christ the Lord as holy, in their heart. Part of this honoring involves being prepared to give reasons (*apologia*) for why we have hope instead of living a life of fear and intimidation (1 Peter 3:13–15).

Therefore, I intend in this book to demonstrate that women's ministries need to include apologetics, that is, training in the defense of Christian beliefs. Women need the transformation that having a trustworthy foundation built on the reasoning of their own belief in God can bring. The women who can say "I believe in God" with intellectual confidence will not only change their own lives, but change the lives of many people. A woman whose conviction in the reality of God is as unshakable as her conviction in the reality of the sun will have a hard time keeping that belief to herself. Someone who is intellectually confident can identify the deficiency of opposing views rather than feeling threatened or intimidated by them, and she can intelligently express the reasons for believing in Christianity.

Let me be clear about what I mean. Intellectual confidence does not mean you had the highest IQ in your graduating class. Rather, it refers to satisfying the rational aspect of your belief in God. All people struggle with what we can know for certain. This struggle does not catch God by surprise. Neither does our searching for truth condemn us before the Truth itself. When I began to have doubts about the

Christian faith, I had to come to the point where I was willing to honestly consider the possibility that God did not exist. It was important for me to understand that God does not mind our questions. The stubborn, hardened heart that is unwilling to consider God is the one rebuked in Scripture—not the heart that questions.[2] Realizing that my doubts arose from observation of people in the church and not on the doctrines of Christianity, I also had to keep my mind open to the possibility of God's existence. I could not allow myself simply to react to the failings of people in the church (which started my doubting, as I will address later).

Throughout this book, I will discuss how a reasoned belief in the reality of God's existence can transform women's lives. It isn't that I've found a new or hidden revelation that will revolutionize the face of theology. I haven't risen above the common man into a superior, loftier realm of philosophy. I am merely equipped with the revelation God has given to all men and women through His creation, through His Word, and through His Son, Jesus Christ. It is through His revelation that I have come to understand God as a real being, and not just as a philosophical concept or traditional religious story.

So why am I bothering to tell you all of this before I begin? A respected friend of mine asked me a couple years ago, "Why would a woman choose to attend a session on apologetics at a women's ministry conference?" Up to that point in my studies, I had never even thought to ask this question. It just never occurred to me that a woman who had a mind to think through her beliefs and the freedom to investigate those beliefs openly wouldn't want to do so. Though I'm certain I gave her quite a list of reasons for why any person, regardless of gender, should be able to defend their beliefs, she was insistent that we need to figure out a way to get women, specifically, in the door of an apologetics session.

I was puzzled by this. During my time as a graduate student in apologetics, I read many books on the topic, and I had never taken special notice of the authors' genders. There was never a time when I

---

2. Jesus confronts Thomas about his unwillingness to believe the reports of Jesus' resurrection (John 20:24–29).

thought, "Oh drat! Another book by a male! Where are the women?" Although I studied diligently, I missed the implications of the sparse presence of women in this vital aspect of the Christian life, and I didn't recognize the untapped potential for a Christian women's movement founded in apologetics. There is a definite need for Christian women to commit to rigorous and public engagement in philosophical and theological thought, especially in the evangelical Christian camp.[3] Furthermore, there is a great need for women who can communicate complex, essential Christian doctrine in an accessible way.

I have come to the point where I am skeptical of my current task: "You aren't seriously thinking of writing an apologetics book targeting women? You tell yourself and others that apologetics is not an area that needs to be gender-specific!" Yet, there is a great deficit in the body of Christ because women are not sufficiently presenting their minds in service to the Lord. The response to apologetics at women's conferences is some of the most excited and passionate I receive in any of my speaking engagements. The response does not seem dependent on whether the congregation is large or small, the people young or old, the church members financially sound or struggling, or if the church is of any particular ethnicity. The reaction seems dependent on the heart of the women in the church.

I recently spoke at a conference in a small church in a small town in Oklahoma. I was concerned about how my presentations would be received. What could an argumentative, suburbanite tomboy from the Northwest possibly have in common with these small town, southern ladies? Just this—these ladies had a great spirit of learning about them and a thirst for the knowledge of God. When I returned home, I received a thank you e-mail from the women's ministry leader exclaiming how excited they are about studying their beliefs in God and "being sure exactly what they believe." She told me their women

---

3. There is a noticeable difference between the number of women who attend the Evangelical Theological Society and Evangelical Philosophical Society meetings and those who attend the more theologically liberal Society of Biblical Literature (SBL) conference. Many more women attend SBL and are active in presentations.

are encouraged to "talk with people and ask them to explain their beliefs and why they believe it." Yes! That's exactly what it's all about!

Jesus explained that the Word of God is received differently by different kinds of people. Some receive the Word with joy, but since they have shallow roots, they fall away when persecution or trials appear. Some who receive the Word let the worries of this life and deceitfulness of wealth choke the Word, making it unfruitful. But the one who received the seed that fell on good soil is the one who hears the word and understands it. That one produces a crop, yielding a hundred, sixty or thirty times what was sown (Matt. 13:18–23). It is my hope that the Word in you will be like the seed that fell on the good soil. The good soil of a pure and wise heart, trained in an understanding of the Word, produces a good harvest. The body of Christ needs all believers to be rooted in the Word so that we may be built up until we all reach unity in the faith and in the knowledge of the Son of God. The body needs the sisters in Christ to return to a deep knowledge of the Word of God.

You are the Christian warriors who are missing-in-action on the battlefield of ideology. So I present my argument—my encouragement—to you, my fellow sisters in Christ, to incorporate the study of apologetics into your women's ministry and into your life. We will look at (1) reasons for knowing why you believe in God; (2) how your beliefs affect your life; (3) how your beliefs affect others; (4) what you can do right now (how to begin discussing beliefs in everyday conversations); (5) what you can do in women's ministries; and (6) the importance of a woman's testimony.

Chapter 1

REASONS FOR KNOWING WHY YOU BELIEVE IN GOD

You just believe in God because that is what you want to be true. You will find arguments and evidence in order to support what you already presuppose about God. If you would just spend the time to look into the arguments against God, you would come to realize he does not exist.

—Anonymous

Ever since I began to write publicly on my belief in God, I have received numerous messages intended to convince me that I have not really looked into why I believe in God. Some of the people are malicious in intent, seeking only to tear down my integrity or, at least, to curb my enthusiasm. Others seem to be more genuine in their concern; not so much caring for me as individual, but concerned that I am spreading untruths about this world. Either way, the person usually assumes that if I were to dig deep into the arguments, I could not honestly profess that God exists and Jesus is God.

The truth of the situation, though, is that in my studied opinion, belief in God is the accurate belief about the reality of life in this universe. God is real. After several years of investigating the doubts that I had about God, I concluded that a thorough account of the universe

17

must assert that God, its creator, exists and Jesus is God in the flesh, who was raised from the dead. These ideas are not a useful delusion that evolved through time. They are not just a result of cultural influence. They are not just believing what my parents believed. They are not just participating in a rich tradition with a nice set of moral values to guide my life. They are not wishful thinking. These ideas convey true knowledge; and this knowledge has changed and is changing my life by leading and guiding my decisions and actions in this world.

A BRIEF BACKGROUND

I was not raised in church or in a very Christian culture. I grew up in Portland, Oregon, where there is not a church on every corner. My young life was not flooded with Christian imagery or ideology, or at least I did not perceive it as such. I have special memories of a childhood filled with watching science and nature shows with my parents. We watched Carl Sagan's *NOVA* and Mutual of Omaha's *Wild America*. We visited museums of natural science, read *National Geographic*, frequented the Portland Rose Gardens amphitheater for its live musical productions, attended plays at Portland Community College, and went camping along the coastline many weekends. Yet, my appreciation of nature and culture grew without any sense of who could bestow such things with intrinsic worth. My mother was a member and leader in the local teacher's union and an avid bookworm. She could spend a full afternoon in the local public library reading newly released books. My dad was a chemical engineer who was also the assistant Brewmaster for Henry Weinhardt's Private Reserve beer (now all my Baptist friends know). Dad had a green thumb and loved tennis and music. I will always remember his quality blueberry and rose bushes. He spent countless hours teaching all of us to play tennis competitively as well as helping me learn to play saxophone. So my childhood was filled with many good things, but it wasn't filled with education about the goodness of the Creator. While I was still very little—too young to remember—my family stopped attending church. My mother tells me they were effectively agnostic by that time.

As for learning outside the home, I was educated in a public school district in the 1980s and 1990s that used expressions like "Winter Holiday" instead of "Christmas Break." The district had already begun to remove religiously charged words from public events. One of my best friends and I helped start a recycling organization, the EARTH club, in our high school, and we attended a few National Energy Education Development workshops and conferences with our biology teacher. Nevertheless, our conservationist work was not based in reverence to the God who ordained humankind to be stewards of His very good creation.

At best, I was unaware of most Christian activities, and church was nearly a complete mystery to me. Since I was an extremely busy teen, I did not have much time to think about things like the question of God. I probably wouldn't even have known where to begin nor thought it worth my time. However, before my high school years ended, I had gained some exposure to the Christian culture: I had participated in a youth camp and I had attended church services with a boyfriend several times.

I highlight these specific aspects of my youth to show that I do not have a background steeped in Christian tradition. On the contrary, while I did not consciously reject Christianity and affirm atheism in those terms, I would have considered myself an atheist, generally indifferent to the existence of God. I became a believer in God after reading through a One-Year Bible given to me by a high school band director. Belief in God seemed much more reasonable from a comprehensive reading of the Bible than from the portrayals of God I had briefly encountered through televangelists and Hollywood (for example, the *Oh, God!* trilogy starring George Burns). I became a follower of Jesus at age twenty after attending numerous church services and understanding the necessity of Christ's salvation for humankind.

During the past few years in ministry, nearly all the atheists and agnostics I have met have assumed that I grew up in the Bible Belt or, at least, in some kind of traditional Christian background. Really, it seems an honest mistake considering that my name sounds more Bible Belt than Pacific Northwest. Even in a recent public debate, a Muslim debater from the United Kingdom said she was a little disappointed that I completely lacked any Southern United States accent, considering my name and current residence in the South. It only takes a quick reading of my biography to see that I come from a non-church, non-religious, non-culturally-Christian background, but I still have received many requests that I should at least explore something other than how I was raised to believe in God and that I should take a more honest look at my belief in God. Yet, this is exactly the task I have already undertaken and which has resulted in my belief in God! So let me share a little bit about why I began to doubt God's existence even after I began to follow Jesus.

About nine years after I became a believer in Christ, I began to have some disturbing doubts about my belief in God. I asked myself: *Why are you a believer in God? Do you really think there is a God or did you just put your faith in something because you needed to at the time? If you really think there is a God, then why aren't you acting like it? How can you truly believe in God and yet practically live your life in the same way as a nonbeliever?* Fueling my doubts were experiences with other Christians whose lives were generally no different from a nonbeliever. They lusted after the same materialistic things; they complained and got angry over trivial matters; they backstabbed and slandered other Christians (especially leaders in the church); and they harbored life-sapping pride. Much of this I experienced directly through the church's women's ministry or with individual women in the church. Worse, I realized my own attitudes and thoughts were not any better. I began to wonder if the faith I proclaimed had any merit whatsoever. Though I still do not remember what gave me the idea, I somehow thought that if God was really the God of the Bible—a perfect creator—then He should have really good answers to my questions and doubts. In fact, He should not just have good answers, but God, Himself, should be the best possible answer to my questions. So I dove into a search for answers to my questions reading not only the arguments for God's existence, but also engaging the opposing arguments.

During this time, I was also considering a master's degree in music education, since I was a band director and had promised myself that I would get a postgraduate degree after I had some experience in my field. As I searched for a degree program and discussed my goals with various universities, I was not satisfied with the level of support or interest to commit to any particular program. I found the lack of opportunity odd, since music education really seemed like the path my life was supposed to go. Even though I was still a young director, I was very active as a leader in the band directing community, and becoming a great band director had been my life's goal ever since I was a sophomore in high school. Although frustrated, I was determined not to give up on my pursuit of a master's degree, and in my continued search for a program I came across an advertisement for a master's degree in Christian Apologetics at Biola University. Though this rarely happens to me, I immediately realized that this was where I would get a master's degree. It was the summer of 2005. I quickly applied to the program, was accepted, and found myself thrust into a whole new world.

Biola's program did not just train me in the doctrines of the Christian faith, but also in the arguments for and against each belief. The students read and interacted with the greatest thinkers from ancient history to the present and examined multiple sides of various arguments. The professors often played devil's advocate with us and challenged any unsubstantiated statements. Furthermore, our professors actively engaged in public debates and/or wrote responses to refutations of their material. I was enthralled! Here I found Christians that defined biblical Christianity as true knowledge about the universe in which we live and that were actively defending that position through evidence and reason. It was the experience at Biola as well as my own doubt about God that taught me to engage both sides of the arguments in order to take an intellectually honest approach to my belief in God.

As this new approach to my faith took root in my life, I brought it back with me to the general church body. Though my teaching was well received, I saw that many people had not attempted to peel back the layers of Christian tradition in their life to see if what they believed was actually true. Many had never deeply investigated the questions, *Why do I believe in God? What are my reasons for thinking God is real and that the Bible is a reliable text inspired by God?* I found that not only did many people lack the answers to difficult questions about God, but they also lacked an understanding of the necessity of finding those answers, even for themselves. This is what kick-started my teaching sessions on the importance of being honest with ourselves about our personal belief in God. This is why at the beginning of this book, I want to deal first with what it means to be honest about our beliefs, and ask you directly if you have ever taken the time to really look into why you are a Christian and why you profess belief in God.

There are three areas to consider when thinking about why this task is so important to the life of the individual Christian and to the life of the church at this point in history: (1) honesty with yourself; (2) honesty with others; and (3) the impact honest investigation of belief has on women's ministry. This book focuses particularly on women's ministry because I have seen many more gentlemen involved in the reasoning of their faith than ladies. I hope to encourage women's ministries to step up to the challenge of responding to our culture by getting back to the root of our beliefs so we can offer a reason for the hope that is within us.[1]

HONESTY WITH YOURSELF

Being completely honest with ourselves is not something that comes easily. Who doesn't like to think that they are okay and their reasoning is solid? Who wants to take the precious little time we have here on earth to dig through the recesses of our minds to root out unjustified beliefs and emotion-controlled ideology? If we do take the time to really look at ourselves and our ways of thinking, will we even be able to bear what we find? This can be one of the most daunting ventures we ever undertake, and it is certainly a painstaking—and painful—process. Yet it is a necessary step in our life in Christ. It is part of the process of peeling away the comfortable layers of our daily activities and thoughts to see what is informing our view of the world. Is our view actually based in a solid belief that God is real and Jesus

---

1. This is in accordance with 1 Peter 3:15.

Christ is the risen Lord and Savior? Has our worldview been hijacked by subtle and not-so-subtle influences of our surrounding culture? Do we even care to know what we actually believe?

It is time to take personal responsibility for our own views and beliefs. It is time to take a hard look at how we individually understand ourselves, the world, and God. Too many times I have heard people say that Christians do not challenge themselves to think through the issues, to do the hard work of understanding their own beliefs, and to ask tough questions.[2] So I challenge you to make a critical assessment of your belief in God in order to be truly honest with yourself first.

As Christians, we are to be lovers of truth. In 1 Corinthians 13's discussion of love, Paul says love "does not rejoice at wrongdoing, but rejoices with the truth" (v. 6). Love delights in discovering what is true. I want to see women who delight in what is true about themselves. We Christian ladies seem generally to trust our own instincts, hunches, and thoughts, even though we affirm the Christian doctrine of the sinful nature. There seems to be a disconnect in our minds that looks something like this: *I am a fallen human being who is prone to corruption, yet I believe I am usually right in all my thoughts and reasoning.* The reality of our current state is that we are not generally a people who meticulously investigate how we know something we believe is true and who love discovering the truth. Thus it is necessary to discuss the truth about our personal beliefs: determining how we arrived at those beliefs and what they mean to us. We must individually return to a rigorous life of the mind; we must commit to the renewing of our minds (Rom. 12:2).

Once we have committed to the renewing of our minds, the next step is to ask ourselves some tough questions. First, *why do I believe in God?* You should have some reasons you can give in response to this question. It is not likely that you will ever be asked the question in this exact manner, but you will encounter the question in some format. In addition, you certainly need to have this topic covered for yourself, as a matter of integrity if you are professing to have the ultimate truth

---

2. Although, since the time that I began writing this book, I have noticed more Christians are getting involved with the reasoning of their beliefs.

about the universe. Second, *how do I know what I believe about God?* This question relates directly to the role of critical reasoning in our lives. We were probably taught at a very young age to think through problems and discover solutions based in reasoning. We were given a scenario we had to investigate using questions: *Who? What? Why? Where? When? How?* Then we were told to draw a conclusion based on the evidence given. These are the same sort of questions we should be asking about what we believe and why we believe it. Third, *what is the source of my information?* Christians are accused of blindly following someone else's teaching and not investigating belief in God for themselves. While this accusation fails to acknowledge that people typically do this with many beliefs (an appeal to authority)—not just belief in God—it is a good reminder that we should be checking for ourselves what we are being taught. Good investigative reporters will go to the primary sources for their information if at all possible. The same method should be true for us as professing Christians. We should go straight to the primary source—in this case, the Bible—and discover all we can about it.

Another aspect of knowing what we believe and why we believe it is to expose ourselves to and interact with the arguments against our position, so that we have considered more than just our own view of the world. But how much of another belief should we read? Isn't it dangerous to expose ourselves to untruths? This was exactly the question asked of me during a question-and-answer panel discussion at an apologetics conference in North Carolina. About halfway through the discussion, I quoted Christian philosopher J. P. Moreland as saying that we should ask people what they have read on both sides of the argument for God's existence. I shared Moreland's recommendation to hold people accountable for grappling with the tough arguments against their own position. When I finished, a gentleman responded, "Well, how much do you think people should read of the opposing viewpoint? Aren't they putting their belief in God in jeopardy by reading that stuff against God's existence?" I responded that a person should have a firm grasp of one's own beliefs (biblical content and context, Christian doctrine, church history) as a part of being a responsible believer. Then I asked the audience this question, "If

God does not exist and therefore belief in God is unable to withstand opposing arguments, then why would you or anyone else believe in Him?" An uneasy silence fell over the room. I intended to encourage honesty and integrity at the deepest levels of our souls, which is vitally important as we talk with others about the truth of Christ. In his first letter to the Corinthians, the apostle Paul says that if it is not absolutely true that Jesus Christ was raised from the dead, then our faith in God is useless and we are giving false testimony (1 Cor. 15:14–15). As I analyzed the interaction of the panel later, I thought, "The comment I made was justified, but how many people in the church can really explain their position? That is probably why the man asked the question. The church doesn't know what it believes, let alone trying to figure out the arguments against its beliefs." This is why we must be brutally honesty with ourselves about what we believe and why: so that we can grow in our own faith in God and move toward maturity in Christ.

I cannot stress the area of honesty with yourself enough. Why would you want to continue to say something is true when you do not have good reason to do so? This is not a question that should take an atheist to ask. You, as a person who professes God as the giver of all truth, should be asking yourself this question before anyone else asks it of you. It is a matter of being responsible with your beliefs. However, let me be careful to say that you can have doubts and believe in God. Just because people have doubts about their faith doesn't mean they have to abandon ship. Doubts are not confirmation that a ship is sinking, but if you question the sturdiness of your vessel, would it not be wiser to examine its soundness before you simply leap into the sea? Even if you still do not have 100 percent confidence that the ship will stay afloat, you also do not have 100 percent confidence that it won't! Do you really need 100 percent confidence that the ship is secure to stay aboard? Would 10 percent, 20 percent, or 40 percent doubt in one's ship be reason enough to jump overboard? No, of course not! You only abandon ship once you are certain the ship is sinking, and as the gales and tempests of this life come, I contend that the more you study, the more you will find that no other ship but the mighty ark of our Christian faith will bear us safely through every challenge and storm. And if we have this confidence in our own faith, the more persuasive we will be as we thoughtfully interact with the ideas and questions of people from other belief systems.

HONESTY WITH OTHERS

One concern I hear repeatedly from non-Christians is that Christians never really seem forthright about their belief in God. When they ask Christians why they believe in God, they receive answers like, "Because that's what I've always believed"; "I don't know. Don't ask that"; or something akin to the old W. C. Fields line, "Go away, kid. You bother me." When pressed further, professing Christians wouldn't answer or even try to answer the questions these folks raised. I wonder how many opportunities to encourage inquisitive minds to further explore belief in God Christians have missed due to their own lack of confidence in this area. How can we expect others to believe the good news if we don't have confidence in our own belief in God? We really should not expect that we will be good witnesses to the truth if we individually are not convinced of what is true.

Being open and honest with others about belief in God came to me more naturally after I was open and honest with myself. Once I was confident with my own decision to believe in God, I was much less apprehensive about talking with others about their views. The world community opened up to me for discussion. I no longer thought, "Gee, I hope they don't think I'm pushing my religion on them." Instead I wondered at others' views of the world and became interested in hearing them tell their stories. I also became very interested in how they arrived at their conclusions. Remember, these are people made in the image of God and sojourners with us in this life—they are not just atheists, agnostics, Muslims, Jews, Mormons, Wiccans, and Jehovah's Witnesses.

The importance of demonstrating a willingness to be completely truthful with others is a vital aspect of our witness. As Christians, we proclaim to have knowledge of the ultimate Truth-Giver. If we cannot demonstrate integrity on the subject of the Truth-Giver, why should anyone believe us? Granted, it is up to each individual to discover what they believe about God for themselves, whether or not the Christians they have encountered have been the best example (see Romans 1 for Paul's admonition that each person can know truth about God). However, as bearers of light, lovers of truth, and representatives of the Creator, we must devote ourselves first to what is true.

Another aspect of this objection to Christianity is that *the church* (as an institution), in its attempt to maintain power over the people, has not always been honest. This is an unfortunate perception of the church, due in part to an imbalanced presentation of the argument (namely, portraying all church leaders as power hungry, rather than balancing this view with those who lead lives of self-sacrifice), and due also to wounds which church members and leaders have inflicted. While the problem of power abuse is common to all humankind throughout time and history, regardless of a religious affiliation, when such immense corruption is associated with a group of people who claim the personal transforming power of God and who claim to know what is righteous, the accusation of hypocrisy is understandable. Since there is a perception of dishonesty in the church among some of the atheistic community, it is our privilege and our responsibility to work actively to change that perception and to help heal the wounds.[3]

At a women's conference in Oklahoma, I presented a talk on the redefining of the term "faith" by our American culture. Afterward, I opened the floor for questions. One of the ladies asked a question to which I did not know the answer. After responding to her that I did not know but that I would find out if she would like to e-mail me, I used the situation at hand to make a quick point. I told the audience, "If you have a similar situation in which you cannot honestly provide a thoughtful response to a difficult question, please do not

---

3. The perception is not that of all atheists, but it is one I have encountered. Bradley R. E. Wright discusses the more generally favorable perception of atheists toward evangelical Christians based in statistical analysis in his book, *Christians Are Hate-Filled Hypocrites . . . and Other Lies You've Been Told: A Sociologist Shatters Myths from the Secular and Christian Media* (Minneapolis: Bethany House, 2010).

make something up or be dismissive. Tell the person you appreciate their question and that you'll try to find an answer and get back with them." I thought this was standard fare, nothing life changing here. Yet, I later spoke with a young woman who told me she had never heard a Christian say "I don't know" in response to a question. She said that she had asked questions but had never felt that her questions were welcomed or that the answers were sincere. She thanked me for those simple words: "I don't know." I asked her if she was a Christian, and she told me that she had decided to follow Jesus as her Lord and Savior. About a week after the conference, I received a note from the women's ministry leader sharing the young woman's story. She was a former atheist who had been invited to the conference by an old high school friend she had recently been back in contact with via Facebook. The young woman had moved toward belief in God after the birth of her daughter, but the conference was the first time that her high school friend had heard her profess Jesus as Lord in a public setting. For this young lady, a lack of honesty on the part of believers had been a huge stumbling block toward acknowledging the existence of God.

Christians need to be humble, realizing that we do not individually, or collectively, have all the answers. But neither does anyone else, no matter what their beliefs. Once we think we have it all figured out, we have taken a God-view of the universe. No one *reasonably* has a God-view of the universe. It doesn't take much investigation to realize our place, but it does take humility—again, no matter what you believe. People outside the church do not trust us at times, because we will not demonstrate modesty of knowledge with them. If we cannot take a truthful position of not having all the answers, we produce some serious side effects, including, but not limited to, (1) thinking we must be right all the time; (2) becoming arrogant, unwilling to listen, unwilling to learn; (3) insecurity, nervousness when talking with people of different views, because we are not sure if we have good answers and we do not know what good answers would even look like; (4) forgetting to hold other people accountable for how they know they are right in their beliefs (which Jesus does), because we become too self-focused in our conversations.

In our interactions with others, we want our honesty to be evident in a natural, informed, and purposeful sharing of reasons for belief in God. The Bible provides two main models of this behavior: Jesus and Paul. Both offered good reasoning to people about what they believed. As Norman Geisler and Frank Zukeran state in *The Apologetics of Jesus*, "Jesus was continually confronted with the need to defend his claims to be the Messiah, the Son of God. So by definition, he was an apologist."[4] Jesus also never asked people to make irresponsible or unreasoned decisions about the afterlife. He willingly offered evidence for His claims. In Luke 7:18–22, John the Baptist sent his own disciples to ask Jesus if He was the promised Messiah or if John should look for another. Jesus responded with His actions. At that moment He healed many sick and diseased and He gave sight to many who were blind. Then, Jesus answered them, "Go and tell John what you have seen and heard: the blind receive their sight, the lame walk, lepers are cleansed, and the deaf hear, the dead are raised up, the poor have good news preached to them" (v. 22). Notice Jesus' response was not, "Tell John he just needs to have more faith in me." Instead, Jesus gave reasonable evidence of His claims to be the promised Messiah. After Jesus' resurrection, Paul made arguments for it nearly everywhere he traveled. The book of Acts reports Paul reasoning in the synagogue and in the marketplaces of the cities to which he traveled. In his famous speech on Mars Hill in Acts 17, Paul laid out a positive case for God's existence, like an opening argument in a lawsuit. He also laid out a closing argument as he stood before King Agrippa in Acts 26, in an attempt to explain the error of his imprisonment.

Paul utilized his knowledge of the surrounding culture and his education in Greek philosophy to testify to the truth of Jesus Christ. In Acts 17:22–31, Paul used the Athenian altar with the inscription "to the unknown God" as a springboard for his discussion about God. He also quoted to the crowd from their own Stoic and Epicurean philosophers in order to show them a generally revealed truth about

---

4. Norman L. Geisler and Patrick Zukeran, *The Apologetics of Jesus: A Caring Approach to Dealing with Doubters* (Grand Rapids: Baker Books, 2009), 11.

God, namely that since we are His creation (offspring), we shouldn't be creating gods of our own. Paul stated, "Yet he is actually not far from each one of us, for 'In him we live and move and have our being'; as even some of your own poets have said, 'For we are indeed his offspring.' Being then God's offspring, we ought not to think that the divine being is like gold or silver or stone, an image formed by the art and imagination of man" (vv. 28–29). Paul then further discussed the revealed truth: "The times of ignorance God overlooked, but now he commands all people everywhere to repent, because he has fixed a day on which he will judge the world in righteousness by a man whom he has appointed; and of this he has given assurance to all by raising him from the dead" (vv. 30–31). Although the poet Paul had quoted was referring to Zeus's offspring,[5] Paul employed this familiar phrase to make an argument for Jesus as the one true God. Paul sought common ground in a shared sense of the nature of God's presence around us. He utilized elements of the culture surrounding him to strike up conversation and to make arguments for God's existence.

Both Jesus and Paul talked with people about belief as a natural outflow of who they were as individuals. Neither of them had a forced or boxed feel to their discussions. In fact, they often seemed quite casual and spontaneous. Jesus could simply walk past a mountain or a tree and use it as an example of a profound truth of reality and of the universe (Matt. 21:21).

If we can focus first in women's ministries on the challenge of being honest with ourselves about belief, my hope is that this change in ministry will facilitate a noticeable transformation in our conversations with others. We will begin to mirror a bit more closely what we see in Jesus and Paul: a natural conversation with God's creation as an expression of our bond with the One who shapes and teaches us. We may never get to the level of ease that Jesus and Paul had in their discourses, but one of our ministry goals, as well as personal

---

5. Aratus, "Phaenomena," in *Callimachus: Hymns and Epigrams, Lycophron and Aratus,* trans. A. W. Mair and G. R. Mair (Loeb Classical Library, vol. 129; London: William Heinemann, 1921). Online text available from: http://www.theoi.com/Text/AratusPhaenomena.html.

life goals, should be to aim for that comfort, figure out why we don't have it, and make changes toward that end. Don't get me wrong—programs that teach Christians how to share their faith are a great resource. However, we also need to recognize and utilize the wealth of cultural sources available to us to be relational in our presentation of the gospel. Truth is truth, and if you honestly believe all truth comes from God, you can use any truth to show the world the reality of God and Jesus as the risen Savior.

Unforced discussion is a part of being honest with others because our communication of the gospel should involve sincere interest in other people and their lives. When we seek to extend the gospel to people or engage them in dialogue about God, we should see them as people instead of as projects. This really is true of any environment the church wishes to create, whether it is a worship setting, a small group, an evangelistic event, or other activity. People are not a means to an end, and especially not a statistical end. People are an end in themselves. When teaching women to engage in discussion about God with atheists and persons of other religious backgrounds, we must emphasize this truth. What we desire is relationship with others, as God desires relationship with us. Yes, we also desire to see people know and trust God, but that relationship is ultimately between the individual and God.

Many women tell me they just don't want to say the wrong thing and mess up another person's chance to come to salvation. My response is to ask why they think they would be responsible for a person's final decision about God. Isn't that responsibility in the hands of the individual themselves? Can you be the Holy Spirit for someone else? Even if we experience some rejection, is it not possible that a seed has been planted which may bear the fruit of faith? Think about how patient God has been with each of us as we continue to learn about truth. Does not God extend the same grace toward others? For some people, it will be a long, hard road toward belief. Our responsibility is not to convince anyone that our reasons to believe in God are true. Rather our responsibility is to become the kind of people from whom reasons naturally and honestly flow. We share what Jesus did for humankind. We share the need for Jesus. We leave the choice to every individual and to the Lord. God knows how to rightly guide and direct His own creation.

APOLOGETICS AND WOMEN'S MINISTRY

The question of why each of us individually believes in God must be handled in women's ministries because it is the most important question we can handle. If women's ministries want to have a greater impact on all generations, then they must deal with such foundational issues as our reasons for belief in God. Women have intellectual doubts about God, not just physical and emotional needs. Women need to know that they have good reason to believe. Women desire deep doctrinal truths that are at least as difficult to grapple with as was their secondary education. When I first became aware that such a thing as women's ministry existed in the church, I had no idea why it was needed. I could not understand why Christians could possibly need a gender-specific ministry to learn about the deep things of God. After participating with women's ministries that seemed to consist of nothing more than frilly events,[6] get-away fellowships, and improving oneself in the ordinary activities of physical life, I was almost entirely turned off to women's ministry altogether. However, apologetics in women's ministry has changed my mind.

For several years, I have served on the Southern Baptist of Texas Women's Ministry team. This came about in part because of a phone call my husband, Roger, made to our state women's ministry leader, Shirley Moses. Roger told Shirley that I had recently been working with the women's ministry team for the Baptist General Convention of Oklahoma, specifically in the area of apologetics. He said, "You really need to meet my wife. I think she could be of great service to the women of Texas." Shirley had never had a husband call her to introduce his wife and suggest that she would be a good addition to Shirley's team. So Shirley called me and I tried for a few hours to

---

6. As stated earlier, I was a tomboy from the Northwest, so I had a bit of a bias against "frilly" things in general. I have since grown more appreciative of the frills.

convince her that I was not right for women's ministry, because my area was apologetics. I did not know at the time how greatly in tune Shirley was with ministry needs in the state of Texas. She persuaded me that the women of Texas needed what I had to offer and that they would receive it well. I was a bit gun shy (Texas pun, of course) because of my previous, though limited, experience with women's ministry. Nevertheless, I gave her the promise of one year on the team.

The first year I served on the team in Texas, I taught women specific apologetics topics, such as "The Evidence of the Resurrection" and "The Problem of Evil." The response to my presentations was quite mixed. Sometimes, I had an overflowing room. Other times, only a few people came. In all cases, I received comments such as, "Where is everyone else? We all need to hear this," and "Wow. That was so exciting!" Yet, the overall response in attendance was unpredictable.

Over the next two years, Shirley and I worked to make the material more attractively titled and organized for women. In addition, we added some topics establishing the need for apologetics. I taught "The Need for the Knowledge of God," "Oprah's False God," "Shouldn't the Reality of God Change Our Lives," and "Asking the Right Questions." Nearly every time I taught, the room was packed or close to capacity. Not only was attendance high, but women began to ask me, "Where do I start in apologetics?" They asked for apologetics Bible studies, books, and ideas for implementing programs in their churches. We would sell out of Wayne Grudem's *Systematic Theology* and Timothy Keller's *The Reason for God,* as well as Greg Koukl's *Tactics: A Game Plan for Discussing Your Christian Convictions.* I started to hear testimonies from women about how they used to be afraid to talk to others about God, but now they discussed hard issues with atheists or Muslims. Other women told me they had no idea there were answers to their doubts about God and the questions they had about biblical texts. The funny aspect of all of this to me was that I wasn't good at handling their excitement. I did not see it coming and did not know what to do with it, because I never expected it from my own prior experience with women's ministry.

The spark ignited in the women's ministries in Texas has only spread. I am now seeing the results of year-long studies in apologetics at individual churches. Women of all ages are excited to dig deep into hard theology, and their discussions on these truths transcend generational lines and cultures. The motivating factor seems to be confidence. Women in the church desire a confidence in their belief in God so that they can "know that they know what they know" and share that knowledge with others. Part of this knowledge is understanding why they personally believe in God, and why they personally think God is real. Another aspect of the apologetics spark that surprised me was the changed lives and transformed hearts. When I studied apologetics, the deep theological study and scrutinizing look at my beliefs really affected my personality and attitude. I am seeing dynamic changes in other women's lives as a result of apologetics studies, as well. Women's lives are being changed due to the incorporation of apologetics into their women's ministries! The change is obviously different for each individual, but the overall excitement for learning about essential Christian doctrines, church history, and philosophical and theological arguments is broad and infectious.

Why do we need to handle this question here and now in our women's ministries? The women in the church are ready for this discussion. They long for the trust in God that comes from a strong, firm relationship in Jesus Christ for which they can aptly articulate reasons. They realize the current ebb of culture is not leaning toward a favorable view of the Christian God, and they want to be able to provide good answers for themselves and others, especially in times of great distress and need. Leaders, too, are looking for ways to incorporate more theological studies, realizing that women may not be able to answer basic questions about their faith in God. Many women have discussed with me family problems, and their own problems, for which the answers are ultimately found in the nature of God, the nature of man, and the nature of Christ. The answers are found in theology. This makes sense if we really believe we are God's creation. As A. W. Tozer stated in *The Knowledge of the Holy*, "Because we are the handiwork of God, it follows that our problems and their solutions are theological. Some knowledge of what kind of God it is that operates the universe is indispensable to a sound philosophy of life and a sane outlook on the world scene."[7] We do have the answers to our questions readily available. We just need to use the abundance of resources we have for growing in our knowledge of God. We must handle this most important question because it has the possibility of affecting every individual woman in our ministries at the core of her belief in God. As ministries equip women to aptly articulate their reasons for belief, to build them up in confidence, and to enable recognition and worship of a real and knowable God, then we will have the makings for deep-seated and sweeping change in the lives of Christian women.

---

7. A. W. Tozer, *The Knowledge of the Holy*, 43.

Chapter 2

YOU WILL LIVE WHAT YOU TRULY BELIEVE

*People may not always live what they profess,
but they will always live what they believe.*
—Neil T. Anderson

Women's ministries today are faced with a growing problem: women are living out what they truly believe. Wait a second, you ask, isn't that a *good* thing? Sadly, it isn't, because many women's beliefs do not stem from biblical truth; thus they experience little growth in the knowledge of God.

At nearly every evangelical women's ministry event I attended over the past four years, the hot topics of discussion have been two: (1) Why aren't women growing in their relationship with God? and (2) Why aren't women sharing their faith? The Barna Research Group's statistical data over the past seventeen years may shed some light on the subject. Its studies show that Christians are becoming less and less a people who desire to know biblical truths:

> The problem facing the Christian Church is not that people lack a complete set of beliefs; the problem is that they have a full slate of beliefs in mind, which they think are consistent with biblical teachings, and they are neither open to being proven wrong

nor to learning new insights. Our research suggests that this challenge initially emerges in the late adolescent or early teenage years. By the time most Americans reach the age of 13 or 14, they think they pretty much know everything of value the Bible has to teach and they are no longer interested in learning more scriptural content.[1]

Does this disturb you as much as it does me? I hope so! Clearly women are not going to grow in their relationship with God if they assume they already learned everything they needed from the Bible as soon as they reached the double digits. Even though some church members, like me, become a Christian in their adult years, if the church keeps ignoring this intellectual carelessness, then the spiritual life of Christians will languish. If no one challenges women, who think that the answers they have to life's questions are wrapped up by their young teenage years, the faith of these women is most likely going to be a bit shallow and their spiritual growth prematurely stunted. In no other field or career is this kind of complacency considered acceptable. To remain cutting edge in any discipline, you would be expected to sharpen your skills and to layer your early conceptions with the mature understanding and insight resulting from continuing study and rigorous application. As Kathleen Norris observes, "Many people who would not dream of relying on the understanding of literature or the sciences they acquired as children are content to leave their juvenile theological convictions largely unexamined."[2] When women stop intellectually engaging with their faith, they are left unprepared for confrontations in their evangelistic efforts; they are bound to encounter questions that they cannot answer and have not even thought

---

1. "Barna Studies the Research, Offers a Year-In-Review Perspective," The Barna Group, last modified 2009, http://www.barna.org/barna-update/article/12-faithspirituality/325-barna-studies-the-research-offers-a-year-in-review-perspective.

2. Kathleen Norris, *Acedia & Me: A Marriage, Monks, and a Writer's Life* (New York: Riverhead, 2008), 114.

about, creating quite a bit of discomfort and perhaps even crises of doubt. When this happens, women can go into "avoidance mode." We can come up with a million other things we have to do for God other than talk with people about our beliefs.

After batting around numerous ideas to get women more involved, from more event-planning to more Bible studies, leaders may fall back on how they can better package the material they have been utilizing or how they can better meet the emotional needs of women. But the fundamental issue goes much deeper. No matter how many programs we plan or how prettily we package the material, our efforts to transform the inward character and passions of women will be ineffective if we do not address the root problem.

The fundamental issue is many women are unaware of their need for a probing study into what they believe is true about God. If they are unaware of their need to search for what is true, they will do nothing to fulfill that need. In his book, *Love Your God with All Your Mind*, Christian philosopher J. P. Moreland tells the story of a woman who lives in his neighborhood who was concerned for the spiritual growth of her son. She said that he routinely asked her a number of questions about her faith that she could not answer. She worried about his growth, as well as whether he would respect her dedication to Christ. Her son had pointed out to her that "she had the time for a number of hobbies, watching television, and so on, so that if getting good answers had mattered to her, she would have gotten them by now. He concluded that her faith must not matter that much to her, because she had not taken the time to wrestle with issues that might show her faith was false."[3]

This story is not unique to Moreland's experience. One of the most common questions I receive at women's conferences is *What do I do about a son/daughter/husband /sister/brother that knows their Bible, but has so many questions to which I have no answers?* Though my response varies with the situation presented, I generally stress the importance of understanding and aptly conveying our own beliefs as a part of a

---

3. J. P. Moreland, *Love Your God with All Your Mind* (Colorado Springs: NavPress, 1997), 135.

lifestyle of faith. Notice in Moreland's story that the son concluded his mother's faith didn't mean very much to her. His perception of her lived-out faith was different from her perception of her beliefs. His conclusion was based in her inability (or reluctance) to probe into deep questions about the truth of her beliefs in God. How could she say God was real if she didn't take the time to wrestle with the relevant issues, especially when she was specifically asked about her beliefs? There is a direct connection between what we do as people of faith and what we actually believe about God. A woman cannot live out trust in God if she doesn't have good reasons to trust in God. She cannot live like God is real if she does not have good reasons to believe that He is.

MOVING TOWARD A SOLUTION

There is much more to trusting God than merely thinking about Him or learning stories about Him. Women have to actually believe that God is a real person with defining qualities. She has to believe that He interacts with the world, and that she can have a real relationship with Him. Without this belief and this relationship, it will be extremely hard to trust God. People do not trust in great stories; they trust in other people. Hebrews 11:6 states, "And without faith it is impossible to please him, for whoever would draw near to God must believe that he exists and that he rewards those who seek him." The Greek word for "believe" here is *pisteuō*, which means "to think to be true, to be persuaded of, to credit, place confidence in."[4] J. Gresham Machen, a great theologian of the early twentieth century, commented on this passage, asserting, "One cannot trust a God whom one holds with the mind to be either non-existent or untrustworthy." He further states, "It is impossible, according to the Epistle to the Hebrews, to have faith in a person without accepting with the mind the facts about the person."[5] A woman must believe that God exists and this belief must

---

4. James Strong, *The Exhaustive Concordance of the Bible*, electronic ed., G4100 (Ontario: Woodside Bible Fellowship, 1996).

5. J. Gresham Machen, *What Is Faith?* (Carlisle, PA: The Banner of Truth Trust, 1991), 47–48.

penetrate the deepest recesses of her mind in order for her to trust Him. If she does not trust God mentally, it logically follows that her behaviors will not display trust in God—she will not attempt to grow in the knowledge of God or seek to evangelize the lost. Instead, her actions will display distrust in God, because she cannot act with reliance on a person whom she does not really know. Just as she requires knowledge *of God* as a truly existing being, she also needs knowledge *about God* in order to have a trusting relationship with Him. People do not normally trust in a person if they have no basic knowledge of that person.

Time and again in my own life, I have struggled with the same old habits and behaviors. I've wondered why is it that I do these things over and over when I profess to believe in a God who is so powerful He can create a universe and conquer death. Certainly this powerful of a God can resolve my proportionally tiny behavioral issues! Then I realize the problem: I *profess* my belief in God, but do I really believe in Him? To be completely honest, sometimes the answer is yes and sometimes it appears to be no. The main reason I have struggled to do the things that Jesus Christ taught me to do is that I have been living as a schizophrenic Christian. Like many others in the church, I have not heeded the exhortation of 1 John 3:18, "Little children, let us not love in word or talk but in deed and truth." I have not trusted enough in the words I profess because I have grasped so very little about the truth of God; thus I lack the resources to demonstrate in my actions that I truly believe in God. In general, women's ministries have not addressed this fundamental issue yet, and as a result, women continue to live ineffective Christian lives.

In this book, I am proposing a new approach to women's ministries that addresses the basic need of women to know the truth about God and thus to trust Him: the study of apologetics specifically for women so that they can learn the truth about God, believe in Him, and live out their faith through their actions. Over the past few years, I have seen this approach transform my own life and the lives of other women.

I have encountered some objections to this proposal in my interactions with people. Let me address these directly. First, some think I am saying we just need more "head knowledge" as opposed to "heart knowledge." In fact, this is a false dichotomy. Christian philosopher J. P. Moreland points out that there is much confusion as to what "heart" means in Scripture. In the Bible, the word *heart* has several meanings. Most of the time, it refers to the whole of a person, including the intellect, will, and emotions. A few times it refers to only the emotions or affections (Rom. 1:24), but it often refers to the mind itself (Rom. 1:21; Eph. 1:18).[6] So when we say "heart knowledge" with reference to the Scriptures, we actually include "head knowledge." If we don't, we generally misrepresent the Scriptures. In no way do I want to sanction faulty reasoning by saying that we should love God more with our emotions than our intellect. This is not the admonition we receive from the Lord, who says to "Love the Lord your God with all your heart and with all your soul and with all your mind" (Matt. 22:37). A woman who loves God with all her mind is loving God with everything that goes along with the mind, including emotions.

Second, some have objected to the statement that I have acted as a schizophrenic Christian. They wonder if I am suggesting that sometimes I do believe and then sometimes I do not believe. The actual problem stems from a trust issue created by my lack of attention to maintaining my beliefs. My sentiment in this regard is best expressed by C. S. Lewis in *Mere Christianity* as he describes how faith is holding on to what your reason has already accepted in spite of your changing moods. In the years following my commitment to Christ, my beliefs were in constant sway with my experiences and emotions because I had not spent enough time to know that I know what I know. Commenting on how his moods impacted his faith in God, Lewis stated, "Now that I am a Christian, I do have moods in which the whole thing looks very improbable: but when I was an atheist I had moods in which Christianity looked terribly probable."[7] My point in this book is to be painfully honest about the current status of women in American evangelical Christianity, not about the

---

6. Paraphrased from Moreland, *Love Your God With All Your Mind*, 60–61.
7. C. S. Lewis, *Mere Christianity* (New York: Macmillan, 1943), 124.

status of women who are philosophy or theology majors studying epistemology.[8] In women's ministries, we do not yet have a desire to learn that is so impassioned as to cause us to question how we know what we know and from where that knowledge has come. We have not yet reached the point of gauging probabilities and percentages of certainty. Rather, we are at the point of stirring up a desperate need for deeper learning about the God we profess. I was at this point of intellectual neutrality for too long. I am still coming out of that place. Women's ministries are on the verge of emerging from this place. It is a place where women say they believe, but they don't have the resources of knowledge to *really* believe. In this place, faith appears to be a fancy or whim or believing apart from reason or evidence.

Finally, a third objection is that I am leaving out the relational, or experiential, knowledge of God as a viable option for knowing God. Again, I do not want to promote poor reasoning from the Scriptures. Knowledge of God in the Bible is never a matter of simply acquiring data. The knowledge of God is comprehensively discussed as knowing a real person.[9] Knowledge of a person is a mingling of the facts you can know about him or her and experiences you've had together that aid your understanding of the person. It is quite difficult to trust someone that you do not know or have a personal relationship with. The mere awareness of cold, hard facts about a person does not equate with a trusting knowledge of that person. This is why Paul could say in Romans 1 that though the heavens declare the glory of God, people have turned away from the truth and worshipped objects of their own creation (vv. 21–25).

Women will only live out genuine faith when they truly believe in God. They will only truly believe in God when they know Him. They will only know Him as they intellectually engage at a deeper level the issues of His existence.

---

8. Epistemology is the study of the nature of knowledge. What do we know? How do we know what we know?

9. Dallas Willard, *Renovation of the Heart: Putting on the Character of Christ* (Colorado Springs, CO: NavPress, 2002), 51.

BACK TO THE BASICS: LEARNING HOW TO THINK

Helping women in our ministries move toward true belief in God begins with teaching them how to think and reason. While we want every woman in our churches to determine what she truly believes and how she acquired those beliefs, we must recognize that this is not an instinctive skill, nor is it broadly taught in the secular culture anymore. We can no longer assume people are "good thinkers" since we are no longer required to study logic at the elementary or high school level or even in the university. Public schools may teach some critical thinking skills, but they don't teach nearly enough to combat the powerful influence of mass media marketing. Our culture overflows with a consumerism that is primarily driven by manipulation and the avoidance of common sense practicality and logical/analytical reasoning. For example, ladies, if you analyze the commercials during your favorite television show, you will begin to notice the numerous commercials designed to make you think you are too old, too heavy, or undesirable without a certain product.[10] This is a manipulative strategy that works, but it is unfortunate that we, who have been given the mind of Christ and thereby have access to the knowledge of reality, have become so susceptible to these bad arguments and false images. But what are we doing to combat this sort of manipulation? We tell women not to listen to these campaigns but instead to trust God. We tell them it is idolatrous to place hope and trust in anything other than God. These statements alone, however, will not effectively overcome such pervasive manipulation.

Most of the women in our churches have not dealt with what their beliefs really are or how they have acquired them. We desperately need to get to the basis of our individual beliefs about God and then consequently about ourselves. This will require us, as the church, to walk alongside our women and teach them

---

10. This is a generalization and would obviously vary with the type of television show. A football game may not have near as many commercials of the described kind.

essential reasoning skills, such as how to recognize hidden premises, counter poor arguments, and identify unfounded beliefs. My hope is that clear reasoning and thinking will become a virtue associated with church-going Christians, but in order for this to happen, the church must get on board with teaching logic and reasoning. Through the process of thinking and reasoning, we will be able to reach a point where we trust our beliefs so that we can stop living as schizophrenic Christians.

ACQUIRING AND MAINTAINING BELIEFS

Being responsible with our beliefs or disbeliefs means first being able to provide reasons why we choose to affirm one belief over another. Then, we must take care of those beliefs. Consider how we bear the burden of responsibility to choose and care for our homes and vehicles. We take time to determine which home or car to choose by considering the facts surrounding each one. We don't just gamble on a possession of such great worth; it is too enormous of a responsibility and there is too much to lose. Not only do we choose our possessions wisely, but we also provide proper maintenance so the house or car remains in good condition. Certain activities must become *routine* with these types of possessions. For the home, we must paint the exterior and clean the interior. For the car we must change the oil and fill the tank with gas.

When it comes to the ownership of beliefs, we must also properly assess and maintain those beliefs to keep them in good condition. In *Mere Christianity*, C. S. Lewis comments, "If you have once accepted Christianity, then some of its main doctrines shall be deliberately held before your mind for some time everyday. That is why daily praying and religious reading and churchgoing are necessary parts of the Christian life. We have to be continually reminded of what we believe. Neither this belief, nor any other will automatically remain alive in the mind."[11] After settling on a belief, then we also need to settle on the fact that we know what we know. Have we challenged this belief? If not, we

---

11. C. S. Lewis, *Mere Christianity* (New York: Macmillan, 1943), 124.

must take steps to thoroughly investigate and examine it. Then, if it still stands, it is time to properly maintain our beliefs through a daily reflection on those beliefs and also a daily utilization of those beliefs as being actually—not just possibly—true and thus meaningfully applicable to our lives. This is when we will see a new creature begin to emerge from the old self. This is when we will see women's ministries begin to transform. When we take responsibility for our beliefs, we will stop living out radical skepticism in our Christianity.

Jesus taught us to be responsible with what we believe. Contrary to what popular American author Mark Twain said, faith in God is not "believing what you know ain't so." While Twain's demeaning caricature of faith has been used for decades to promote antireligious sentiments, does it really portray the belief in God described in the New Testament? Not at all! In fact, Jesus strongly rebukes those who are irresponsible with their belief or disbelief.

In Matthew 22:23–33, Jesus is approached by the Sadducees, who ask Him a theological question concerning marriage in the resurrection (the Sadducees did not believe in the spiritual realm or in the resurrection).

> The same day Sadducees came to him, who say that there is no resurrection, and they asked him a question, saying, "Teacher, Moses said, 'If a man dies having no children, his brother must marry the widow and raise up children for his brother.' Now there were seven brothers among us. The first married and died, and having no children left his wife to his brother. So too the second and third, down to the seventh. After them all, the woman died. In the resurrection, therefore, of the seven, whose wife will she be? For they all had her" (Matt. 22:23–28).

In order to avoid the absurdity of a woman with seven husbands in the resurrection, the Sadducees thought Jesus would either have to renounce Moses' teaching on marriage or renounce the resurrection. So they attempted to set an intellectual trap for Jesus concerning the law of God. But instead of taking their bait, notice how He replies: "You are wrong, because you know neither the Scriptures nor the power of God" (v. 29). Jesus asserts that these religious teachers are uninformed on their own beliefs. He then goes on to show them how they are wrong: "For in the resurrection they neither marry nor are given in marriage, but are like angels in heaven" (v. 30). The Sadducees wrongly assumed that the conception of afterlife was merely a better version of this life where our interpersonal relationships will be the same. This displayed their ignorance of the biblical position on the resurrection.[12] Since these men only accepted divine authority of the Pentateuch—the first five books of the Old Testament—and rejected the rest of the Hebrew Scriptures, Jesus refutes them using the very books they profess to know by quoting from Exodus 3:6, "And as for the resurrection of the dead, have you not read what was said to you by God: 'I am the God of Abraham, and the God of Isaac, and the God of Jacob'? He is not God of the dead, but of the living" (Matt. 22:31–32). Notice Jesus' statement: "Have you *not read what was said to you by God?*" Jesus demanded accountability for their disbelief in the resurrection in accordance with their own Scriptures. There is no praise to be found here for believing, or disbelieving, irresponsibly. Jesus additionally states that in combination with their ignorance, the Sadducees do not know the power of God. They cannot trust God—and experience or realize His power—because they do not know Him. Jesus' point here can be very effective for our ministries. Instead of just teaching the stories and what life lessons we might learn from them, we also need to instruct our women to handle beliefs with responsibility, examining them carefully, so that we may learn to trust God and experience His power.

Perhaps you are thinking, *So are you saying that we should stop our questioning after we profess faith? Isn't that exactly the accusation non-Christians use against Christians—that we aren't "allowed" to ask questions of our faith?* Yes, that is the accusation and, no, I'm

---

12. Essentially, the Sadducees built a strawman argument, in which they misrepresented Jesus' view of the resurrection in order to refute more easily the concept of resurrection.

not suggesting we completely stop asking questions. I am specifically addressing the radical hyper-skepticism of the culture in which American Christians, and more broadly Western civilization, are immersed that has so greatly affected our ministries. This skepticism renders our churches less like centers of hope for humankind and more like country clubs with private get-togethers. As Christian philosopher, Dallas Willard, poignantly remarked, "We live in an age in which it is considered a virtue to disbelieve and a vice to believe."[13] We have become so radically skeptical that we think the intelligent person is one who constantly questions everything; we don't understand that "you can be as dumb as a cabbage and still ask 'Why?'"[14] Willard declares that not only should you be skeptical of your beliefs and believe in your skepticism, but you should also believe in your beliefs and be skeptical of your skepticism. Once you get to a point where you have grappled with certain issues over and over and have come to a conclusion, you should stand confidently on that conclusion while being ready to listen to and openly consider other viewpoints. This does not mean we shut down inquiry or brush aside questions with which people are honestly struggling. It does mean that it *is* intellectually respectable to believe in God and to trust that belief. It is through trusting in a real God—real trust in a real person—we are going to see changes in how we will live out that trust.

GROWING IN THE KNOWLEDGE OF GOD

When I first became a Christian, I was on fire to learn. I used to walk two miles to the church every Sunday evening, rain or shine, pushing my baby daughter in a stroller, to go to discipleship courses. This was in addition to my regular church attendance on Sunday mornings and Wednesday evenings. Indeed, my dedication to learning now

---

13. Dallas Willard, "Morally Responsible Skepticism," (lecture, Indiana University, Bloomington, IN, December 31, 2005) http://www.veritas.org/Media.aspx#!/v/134.

14. Ibid.

sounds somewhat like the makings of an old joke! After a couple years, though, the busyness of life began to take over. School, work, parenting, and family constantly fought for first place in my life. I fell into that old trap of complacency, telling myself, "I'm a Christian. Jesus loves me. I'm okay." Yet after years of the hurtful experiences with other Christians—such as gossip, slander, fighting, condemnation, manipulation, and self-righteousness—I had a set of unpleasant experiences, which eroded the foundation of my Christianity, my belief in God. I didn't have any real arguments and evidence against God's existence, but rather the questions and doubts in my mind arose because I had not been keeping up with the proper care of my beliefs, and so I had failed to substantially grow in my knowledge of God. Since I had not advanced in learning about my belief by studying the deeper doctrines and philosophy such as the necessity of Christ and the problem of evil, I greatly lacked the resources to address the problems of this life. Throughout my own journey for answers, I discovered much of the body of Christ lacked these deeper resources as well. It is the spiritual change I have found in myself and in others, who are well versed in biblical truth and apologetics, that fuels my passion to push others to delve more deeply into the rationality of faith.

One challenge my husband and I have encountered during our sixteen years of ministry comes from church members who claim, "I just have a simple faith," in response to hard theological or philosophical questions we have posed to them. Normally, this response is given as an answer for why that person does not study difficult Scripture passages. The answer always bothers me because I don't understand why a person wouldn't want to jump into the deep waters of learning about their belief in God. Also, when I would discuss objections to the Christian faith, I would hear another response, particularly from women in the church, which was "I just tell people, 'Jesus loves you.'" Though I believe people who use these phrases generally mean well, both of these statements are misguided considering our current lack of scriptural knowledge in the body of Christ.

The idea of a "simple faith" is most often pulled out of context from the story of Jesus and the little children: "Let the children come to me; do not hinder them, for to such belongs the kingdom of God. Truly, I say to you, whoever does not receive the kingdom of God like a child shall not enter it" (Mark 10:14–15). However, Jesus addresses the attitude of the person here, not the person's depth of understanding about God. Jesus emphasizes the importance of a person being open and trusting like a child in order to come into the kingdom of God. This childlike attitude is a humble acknowledgement of one's own need for a greater person's help. To use this verse as a way to shirk one's Christian education is to use it out of context. In fact, children are naturally very receptive toward learning. A stubborn heart that is not willing to continue education and take correction is not a person with childlike faith but rather a fool (Prov. 1:7). The apostle Paul instructs the church in Ephesus to grow in the "knowledge of the Son of God" for the purpose of maturity and unity in Christ "so that we may no longer be children, tossed to and fro by the waves and carried about by every wind of doctrine, by human cunning, by craftiness in deceitful schemes" (Eph. 4:13–14). The author of Hebrews expresses similar frustration with Christians who continue to be spiritual infants: "For though by this time you ought to be teachers, you need someone to teach you again the basic principles of the oracles of God. You need milk, not solid food, for everyone who lives on milk is unskilled in the word of righteousness, since he is a child" (Heb. 5:12–13). We will not find any support from the biblical text to say we don't grapple with difficult theological issues because we have a simple or childlike faith.

The Barna Research Group has studied the area of biblical literacy for many years. In a survey on their research for 2009, the Group noted that fewer than one out of every five persons claiming to be born again adults (19 percent) has a biblical worldview, a statistic which has not changed in the past thirteen years.[15] The only

---

15. "Barna Survey Examines Changes in Worldview Among Christians over the Past 13 Years" The Barna Group, last modified March 6, 2009, http://www.barna.org/barna-update/article/21-transformation/252-barna-survey-examines-changes-in-worldview-among-christians-over-the-past-13-years. "For the purposes of the survey, a 'biblical worldview' was defined as believing that

good news I can find in this statistic is that it has not changed for the worse. The bad news is the statistic itself. Fewer than one out of every five evangelical Christians uses the Bible as a meaningful or trustworthy source for living their lives. The study further notes that only half of those who identified themselves as Christians (not necessarily evangelicals) firmly believe that the Bible is totally accurate in all of the principles that it teaches. Notice the survey did not say "accurate in all of the minute details and facts," but just in *the principles* that it teaches. Half of the people who call themselves Christian aren't sure if the Bible is teaching accurate principles? Why are these people taking on the title of "Christian" if they do not think Christianity is true? Apparently many of us are trying to get by in Christianity without doing any serious study into what we believe or why we believe it. This kind of irresponsible belief will manifest itself in our daily living.

In *The Knowledge of the Holy*, A. W. Tozer laments the serious lack of understanding in the church: "It is not a cheerful thought that millions of us who live in a land of Bibles, who belong to churches and labor to promote the Christian religion, may yet pass our whole life on this earth without once having thought or tried to think seriously about the being of God."[16] We need to pause and give some time and depth of thought to Tozer's statement. As American Christians, we live in the land of plenty. We have the means necessary to access more than enough information to reflect on the nature of God. Yet are we choosing to use our time to become knowledgeable in our beliefs? No. In fact, I fear many people in the church no longer enjoy rigorous theological learning at all. Some individuals may be burned out from an educational environment that taught them to score well on tests rather than be filled with a lifelong love of learning. Others take their

---

absolute moral truth exists; the Bible is totally accurate in all of the principles it teaches; Satan is considered to be a real being or force, not merely symbolic; a person cannot earn their way into Heaven by trying to be good or do good works; Jesus Christ lived a sinless life on earth; and God is the all-knowing, all-powerful creator of the world who still rules the universe today. In the research, anyone who held all of those beliefs was said to have a biblical worldview."

16. A. W. Tozer, *The Knowledge of the Holy* (New York: Harper Collins, 1961), 42.

dislike and distrust of learning to the extreme, even denigrating philosophers and theologians in sermons and presentations in church. I have one Christian friend who says that he doesn't read books at all. I want to ask him, "Isn't the Bible a book?" On the contrary, we, as His children, should possess an awe, wonder, and receptivity to learning about God. These are marks of a Christian; these are not just activities we might do if we can find the time.

LIVING WHAT WE BELIEVE

Occasionally I meet a young Christian who will vent about her struggles to live in a godly way and the crises of doubt her failure causes her to have, "How can Christianity be true, if I keep sinning? If God is real and all-powerful, then why doesn't He change me? I thought I was supposed to be different by now. Why can't I live what I believe?" In response to these kinds of concerns, I generally begin by asking, "What do you believe?" Then the person rattles off some basic Christian beliefs such as "Jesus is the Son of God," "I'm saved by the grace of God," and so on. Yet when pressed to explain these beliefs, sometimes the individual becomes flustered and just says, "I don't know how to explain those things. I just know they are true." At this point, I gently but firmly point out that clearly she does *not* really know what she believes yet. This type of person may have picked up on some "Christianese," but since she does not grasp what these statements actually mean, there has not been a noticeable alteration of her worldly character. Her doubts stem from her failure to change, which in turn results from her lack of knowledge. If she does not make a concerted effort to understand what she believes, she will never live out in action what she claims to believe. The only way for her to become more confident in these doctrines is to study them. So I consistently urge young Christians with these kinds of struggles to read the biblical texts and to check out discussions of these doctrines in a systematic theology book. I'm sharing these experiences to show exactly where we are missing a great opportunity in women's ministries. Women can only live according to what they truly believe, so to experience transformation, we must attend to the life of the mind with a renewed passion.

In Proverbs 4:5–9, Solomon, like his father before him, exhorts his sons to passionately pursue wisdom:

> Acquire wisdom! Acquire understanding!
> Do not forget nor turn away from the words of my
>   mouth.
> Do not forsake her, and she will guard you;
> Love her, and she will watch over you.
> The beginning of wisdom is: Acquire wisdom;
> And with all your acquiring, get understanding.
> Prize her, and she will exalt you;
> She will honor you if you embrace her.
> She will place on your head a garland of grace;
> She will present you with a crown of beauty (NASB).

The obvious application of these instructions is to grow in our knowledge of God. However, let's examine the assertions of Proverbs more deeply. Wisdom guards a person and watches over her; so, if we are confident of the knowledge we have and the discernment to live wisely according to the truth, then, knowing that wisdom guards our steps, we should not live worrisome lives. Yet do not many women in our ministries worry about various commitments and concerns on a day-to-day basis? When was the last time our charge to women for getting their lives ordered and for feeling comforted in troubling times was to acquire wisdom? When was the last time we probed a disquieted and anxious person about her search for pursuit of wisdom? Solomon's instruction here is that wisdom is not just for "head knowledge," but that wisdom brings all of those things we desire: exaltation, honor, grace, and beauty. Wisdom is what watches over and guards us.[17]

Notice, though, that we cannot just seek after wisdom; we must love wisdom. Solomon makes the claim that we must be the kind of people who naturally love truth and instruction and the application of such to

---

17. Wisdom is defined as knowledge utilized in a person's life (experience and knowledge).

our daily lives. Then he says that even the very beginning of wisdom itself is to acquire wisdom. This enigmatic remark seems to imply that the beginning of wisdom requires the realization that you do not have wisdom and must pursue it; the act of pursuing wisdom demonstrates wisdom! This adventurous pursuit of wisdom is not simply the accumulation of disinterested facts about God, but rather the pursuit of a profound understanding of these truths. Spiritual wisdom takes hold of your very being, illuminating your heart, soul, and mind so that you cannot help but experience transformation. It is a lightbulb moment, an *aha!* moment, when the Spirit within you testifies that you are no longer capable of being completely the same person you were prior to that moment. Dallas Willard best expresses this concept, "To think of God for who he is, is to lapse into worship."[18] True understanding creates the reverence that produces real change.

In Proverbs 3:15, Solomon avows that "Nothing you desire can compare with [wisdom]." What a radical expectation of the transformation of believers in God! Notice that a contrast is being made between wisdom and all the things of this world. We are supposed to pursue the wisdom of God with all our mind and with everything we have, but there is a cost. We must get rid of everything that hinders us from understanding. The pursuit of wisdom requires diligence and supernatural grace as we forsake our former fidelities and competing loves and as we forcefully jettison the commitment to sin and folly in order to make room for the One who alone is wise to dwell within us and shape our lives.

Jesus makes radical claims about the kind of personal transformation He expected of His followers. In Luke 9:59–62, Jesus calls two men to follow Him. One replies, "Let me first go and bury my father." The other one replies, "I will follow you, Lord, but let me first say farewell to those at my home." Jesus' responses may seem too harsh to us to be real. Jesus answered, "Leave the dead to bury their own dead. But as for you, go and proclaim the kingdom of God," and "No one who puts his hand to the plow and looks back is fit for the kingdom of God." Pastor David Platt, in his book *Radical: Taking Back Your*

---

18. Dallas Willard, *Renovation of the Heart: Putting on the Character of Christ,* 107.

Faith from the American Dream, says of these stories that the dangerous reality the passages convey is Jesus, in this parable, actually calls us to give up everything and follow Him, even to the point of leaving behind family and friends. Yet we don't want to believe God would ask us to do such a thing, so we attempt to rationalize these passages away and we turn our belief in Jesus into something unbiblical and inconsistent with reality. We change our belief about God to an untruth that is more comfortable, such as "I don't want to offend others by sharing my belief in Jesus, since religion is a private matter." Belief in God, however, is radically different from the beliefs that speak soothing words to our sinful nature. This is where much of our problems arise with women's ministries: we desire comfort over truth.

Instead of digging deep into our theological and philosophical questions, we may be living out a bogus belief in Jesus that is all about personal comfort and peace. It is not the truth about reality. If we want women's ministries to be effectual in aiding the transformation of people's lives, we must address some hard, fundamental issues. This means will we have to stop behaving as though God exists to meet our emotional needs and personal goals, and get serious about nourishing our minds and affirming that we exist to learn the truth about Him so that we can live for His glory.

Remember that Jesus lived like He did because He knew the Father intimately, sought after instruction from His youth, and was willing to take radical action to center His mind on God's truth in order to contend with the world and the flesh. When He had been fasting for forty days, He refused the tempter by saying, "It is written, 'Man shall not live on bread alone, but on every word that proceeds out of the mouth of God'" (Matt. 4:4, NASB). In a physically-weakened, energy-depleted state, Christ yet had immense power because of His grasp of fundamental reality. His statement was not a nice euphemism, but a foundational truth about life. What we know about God affects what we believe about God. In turn, we live out those very beliefs and share them through our actions with the world. Rather than treating the study of God as a luxury item with too high a price tag for our intellect and our time, we must hunger for knowledge of God and strive for it as the ultimate necessity for survival, more essential than the very food we eat.

Chapter 3

YOUR BELIEFS AFFECT OTHERS

*Our attitudes, words, and actions, and oftentimes
even our private unspoken thoughts, tend
to have an effect on those around us.*
—Jerry Bridges, Respectable Sins

When my daughter, Emily, attended elementary school, she used to ride the bus every day after school to the middle school where I taught band. She would come into my office in the band room and begin to share her day with me. I would like to say that I lovingly listened and interacted with her, but the truth is, she usually ended up getting in trouble with me. I was tired, cranky, and had a lot of work to get done before we could head home. Emily pointed out to me that she got into trouble more frequently after school than any other time. I remember responding that she was correct, and saying I'd try to work on improving my demeanor. However, it seemed that no matter how much I tried, she continued to catch my ill-begotten wrath.

During my second semester in the Christian apologetics program at Biola University, Emily carefully broached the subject of my after-school behavior again. What she said drastically changed the way I viewed myself as a Christian and as a parent. Emily said, "Mom, I have noticed that since you began your school, you have been a lot less petty." Emily specifically mentioned that my anger at her small offenses had greatly diminished. I did not even know she knew what the word *petty* meant! She further told me that I seemed to have my priorities better in place. I can only imagine how she must have feared my response as she cautiously shared her thoughts with me. What really caught my attention about her comments was noting the only major factor that had changed in my life: the study of apologetics. I enrolled in the program at Biola to gain better insight to the questions I had regarding my belief in God. What I did not expect was that, as I studied about my belief in God, my attitude might begin to change noticeably. The real impact of Emily's observation and her comments to me came as I considered the source of this transformation: the study of the knowledge of God. I realized that using my time to think about the reality of God and who He is changed the way I treated others, even in the parenting of my own child. As my beliefs became stronger and more deeply rooted, I began interacting with my community in a more loving way.

THOUGHTS LEAD TO ACTIONS

Jesus taught that because our thoughts lead to actions, we should focus our attention on disciplining our thoughts. Two passages from the Sermon on the Mount make this clear. The first is Matthew 5:21–22, "You have heard that it was said to those of old, 'You shall not murder; and whoever murders will be liable to judgment.' But I say to you that everyone who is angry with his brother will be liable to judgment." The passage goes on, "You have heard that it was said, 'You shall not commit adultery.' But I say to you that everyone who looks at a woman with lustful intent has already committed adultery with her in his heart" (Matt. 5:27–28). Notice that in both passages, it is not just the outward actions that are problematic, but the thoughts of the individual are problematic as well. While obviously both murder and adultery are worse than anger and lust, it is anger and lust that cause the murder and adultery.

D. A. Carson, a professor of New Testament studies, states, "Where the heart is not right, drastic action is needed to correct it *before* it results in outward sin."[1] Jesus' teaching emphasizes that our thoughts and attitudes have an effect not only on ourselves, but also on those around us. He follows up His teaching with a metaphorical saying that if your right eye causes you to stumble, you should gouge it out; or if your right hand causes you to stumble, you should cut it off and throw it away (see Matt. 5:29–30). While Jesus is not calling for a literal surgical removal, He is emphasizing that unless we do something drastic, our thoughts will work out into actions against others. Don't overlook this example just because adultery or murder may not be your problems.

Our thoughts—yours and mine—lead to our actions. Our actions will always affect people around us. It is not possible for us just to "be an individual" and to "have it our way" without affecting someone else. This includes our thoughts! Yet, how often do we consider that our thought life may be causing the issues? This is where Jesus' teaching differs so greatly from other views, even modern views. He correlates the thoughts and intentions to the action itself, teaching us to understand that outward displays cannot ever change the inner person. In fact, the opposite is true: the unseen inner person is revealed in the outward displays.

Islam's prophet Muhammad once said, "After me I have not left any *Fitnah* (trial and affliction) more harmful to men than women."[2] In Islamic theology, the beauty of women can be hugely detrimental to men, who may lust after any visible body part, even those as seemingly innocuous as faces and hair. The Qur'an commands that these things therefore must be veiled (Surah 24:30–31).[3] Islam teaches that the covering of a woman's exterior beauty will alleviate

---

1. G. J. Wenham et al, eds., *New Bible Commentary: 21st Century Edition,* 4th ed. (Leicester, England: InterVarsity Press, 1994), ad loc. Matt. 5:17.

2. Sahih al-Bukhari, number 5096, Khan translation. Fitnah is also defined as "temptation."

3. "And say to the believing women that they should lower their gaze and guard their modesty; that they should not display their beauty and ornaments except what (must ordinarily) appear thereof; that they should draw their veils over their bosoms and not display their beauty" (Surah 24:31).

the problem of lust and protect women from harassment (Surah 33:59).[4] However, can this action solve the problem of lust inside a man's heart? Remember Jesus taught that the problem stems from thoughts, which lead to actions. A women's covering may help by not provoking a man's thoughts or by not directing his attention onto those thoughts. However, the problem still lies in the man's intentions and thought life. Even if she veils, a man can continue to dwell on images of women in his mind or fantasize about a woman who is veiled. Muhammad's example on how to deal with lustful desire when tempted by another woman was to go have sexual intercourse with his wife.[5] Again, however, this may temporarily alleviate the problem, but it does nothing to solve the attitude of lust. The man must come to terms with his own lust and do something radical to change before his evil thoughts give birth to evil actions.[6]

Modesty is encouraged in Christian scriptures, but it is less about preventing sin and more about not overshadowing the inward virtue and good works of one who has been transformed in nature to do what is good and right (see 1 Tim. 2:9; 1 Peter 3:4). As the *Tyndale Concise Bible Commentary* states, "Jesus called His hearers to move from external obedience to an obedience motivated by the law written upon the heart."[7] Yet, the problem is not just about what we are thinking, but also how we are thinking. Philosophy professor Dallas Willard comments, "The prospering of God's cause on earth depends upon his people thinking well. . . . Bluntly, to serve God well we must think straight; and crooked thinking, unintentional or not, always favors evil. And when crooked thinking gets elevated into

---

4. "O Prophet! Tell thy wives and daughters, and the believing women, that they should cast their outer garments over their persons (when abroad): that is most convenient, that they should be known (as such) and not molested" (Surah 33:59; Yusuf Ali translation).

5. Sahih Muslim, book 8, number 3240 (Siddiqui translation).

6. Note that not all Muslims will know this teaching nor accept it.

7. Robert B. Hughes and J. Carl Laney, *Tyndale Concise Bible Commentary* (Wheaton, IL: Tyndale, 2001), 401.

group orthodoxy, whether religious or secular, there is always, quite literally, 'hell to pay.'"[8]

As we saw in the Sermon on the Mount, what we think about we will eventually act upon. In conjunction with this idea, *how* we think will also be a determining factor in how we act. Poor reasoning leads to decisions and actions based in poor reasoning. As Willard commented, when poor reasoning becomes the basis for group orthodoxy, the resultant actions can be devastating for our communities. In Hosea 4:6, the prophet exclaimed that God's people are destroyed for a lack of knowledge about God. This basic idea is covered over and over throughout the Bible in warnings to grow in the knowledge of God and through commands to gain wisdom. God's people are supposed to be rooted in knowledge and act upon that knowledge for the express purpose of abounding in love.

Paul prayed for the Philippian Christians, "And this is my prayer: that your love may abound more and more in knowledge and depth of insight, so that you may be able to discern what is best and may be pure and blameless for the day of Christ, filled with the fruit of righteousness that comes through Jesus Christ—to the glory and praise of God" (Phil. 1:9–11, NIV). Love here is guided by knowledge and depth of insight. Christians often talk of how we need to demonstrate great love to the world. But what does that love look like? What is a tangible way to describe this kind of love? D. A. Carson answers that love "needs to be more than blind enthusiasm. It needs to be guided by *knowledge and depth of insight* (cf. Col. 1:9), 'the gift of true discrimination,' a sensitivity to the truth of God and the needs of others, and the understanding of one's situation."[9] We should not believe that we can act in a loving manner separate from the life of our mind. Love abounds as we mature in Christ, a sentiment expressed so clearly by the apostle Paul to the Philippians. One of the vital reasons we must become good critical

---

8. Dallas Willard, *Renovation of the Heart: Putting on the Character of Christ*, 105–6.

9. G. J. Wenham et al., eds., *New Bible Commentary: 21st century ed.*, 4th ed., ad loc. Phil. 1:8.

thinkers is so we can become those who flourish in love, spreading wisdom through godly discernment.

SEEING "DEPTH OF INSIGHT" IN ACTION

What would happen to our women's ministries if we began to focus on each individual's "depth of insight"? If we approached learning about God much like a teacher approaches a student in school, seeking to enable the student to master the material, how would this begin to change our ministries?

I had the privilege of meeting a group of women who had already begun such transformation when I spoke at their ladies' retreat. This group was from a mid-size church in northern Texas. They invited me to address women at their annual event on the topic of apologetics. The first night I gave my presentation on the need to go deeper in the knowledge of God along with a defense of why they should incorporate training in apologetics. Normally, the reaction I get from women's ministries is an *aha* or lightbulb moment. Not with this group. These ladies had already started a fire in their ministry to learn the "hard stuff" about God. After my first session, a younger woman came to me and said, "Mary Jo, we certainly enjoyed your talk tonight, but I can tell you that we are ready for this material. You can go as deep as you like into your apologetics topics. We want this." I was astounded. I had been speaking at women's events all over Texas for two years with the express purpose of creating a thirst for theology and apologetics. That night I met women who already understood the message and were thirsty for everything I had to offer. I was excited.

In addition to ramping up their study of God, these ladies began to hold each other accountable for their reasoning, attitudes, and actions with one another. I heard stories about younger ladies who were mentored by older ladies, and I noticed a genuine excitement to fellowship with one another. So I had to ask about where their ministry had focused its efforts to develop such loving, and learning environment. Their reply was in the deep study of God—essential Christian doctrines, attributes of God, and some harder theological issues as well. They used many familiar means to achieve their goal: mentoring, retreats, and Bible studies, but in all of them, the prize of knowledge was emphasized and the focus was on learning.

By the second night, I had gained a better understanding of what this group expected. After lavishing praises on them for their hunger to go deeper, I dove into a presentation on how to have everyday conversations that lead others toward God. When I talked about having reasons for why you believe in God, I told the women I would share some apologetic arguments with them. As I spouted off the names of arguments for God's existence—the moral law argument, the kalām cosmological argument, the teleological argument, the evidence for the historicity of the resurrection—a woman on the center aisle called out, "How do you spell that?" As soon as I began to respond, a majority of the group focused downward on their notebooks spelling out each argument title. In this group were about a hundred women of different ages. They didn't scoff at the tough terminology. They didn't denigrate hard theology and philosophy. They wanted to know all these things for themselves. And the most prevalent characteristic of the group that I observed for three days was their great joy and love for one another. They were living out their belief in a mighty, eternal, all-powerful God . . . and it showed.

The desire for learning was not the only remarkable trait this group of women exhibited. I also observed great prayer warriors, who displayed a humble and trusting attitude toward God. Many of the women had been through trying and painful experiences and had to reconcile their beliefs with those trying times. These different traits may hold true in many women's ministries, but what stood out the most in this group was their love of learning hard theology. This love gave their group an air of childlike expectancy to grow through encountering the Word of God.

I do not wish to convey the idea that if we all just learn doctrines of God, our ministries will completely transform. This is certainly mistaken and could be quickly disproved. As the British theologian Alister McGrath conveys, "A theology that is untested against the harsh experience of the world will always be prone to doubt and despair."[10] My goal is to recapture the importance of the intellectual part of the Christian life that has diminished much over the years. I long for women's ministries to revere wisdom as a vital aspect of Christian living. Experience and knowledge combine to lead us to wisdom, which is not the same as having all the answers. It is a wise person who learns from experience what they can and cannot know and then utilizes this wisdom in daily actions. As we grow in knowledge and wisdom, as Paul said so well in Philippians, we can also abound in love.

THE UNITY AND HEALTH OF THE BODY OF CHRIST

The church is a spiritual community, as well as a physical one. We are united, as one, in the Spirit through Christ. Paul wrote that by one Spirit we are baptized into one body, though we are many members (1 Cor. 12:12–13). To the Ephesians he wrote to be diligent to keep the unity of the Spirit in the bond of peace, because there is one body and one Spirit (Eph. 4:1–4). One of Paul's main concerns was the unity of the church. Since we are spiritual beings, we must understand we have a spiritual responsibility to the community. The unity of the church can be disrupted through our attitudes of arrogance, false humility, anger, pride, and selfishness. In fact, we don't need to do anything physically to disrupt the unity; we can just harbor jealousy or contempt for another person. This is enough to upset the church's harmonious bond in Christ. Yet, as Jesus taught, such thoughts will work their way out into destructive actions toward one another. The passage in 1 Corinthians 12 further affirms the spiritual side of our bond: "But God has so composed the body, giving greater honor to the part that lacked it that there may be no division in the body, but that the members may have the same care for one another. If one member suffers, all suffer together; if one member is honored, all rejoice together" (vv. 24–26).

---

10. Alister McGrath, *The Passionate Intellect: Christian Faith and the Discipleship of the Mind* (Downers Grove, IL: InterVarsity Press, 2010), 67.

Why emphasize this spiritual bond so much in a chapter on how our beliefs affect others? Women in the church need to be reminded of the powerful nature of our thought lives. Generally, we show little regard for how our thoughts and attitudes disrupt the spiritual unity of the body—as if the Spirit, and the unity He gives, was something that simply did not exist. But our thoughts do affect the lives of others! Those things done in secret do work themselves out into the light of day through attitudes and actions. This is a reality of the Christian view of the nature of man.

Our devastating situation in this life is that sin is a spiritual reality ruining everything, including our minds. In Cornelius Plantinga Jr.'s book, *Not the Way It's Supposed to Be*, he describes the effect of sin as a "despoiling" of our human nature. The imagery Plantinga uses is that of the stripping of an animal of its hide or an army of its weapons and provisions. Basically, this despoiling is the removal of that which protects a person from outside invaders or an animal from its guts spilling out. To despoil is to "wreck integrity or wholeness, to strip away what holds a being together and what joins it to other beings in an atmosphere of hospitality, justice, and delight."[11] Poor thinking as a result of sin robs us of the ability to protect our minds from the invasion of false ideas. Paul understood the reality of this debased reasoning when he proclaims in Romans 1 that through debased and foolish thinking all sorts of evils come from people. He consistently reminded the early followers of Christ to give their minds to thinking on true and honorable things (Phil. 4:8) and to grow in the knowledge of God (Eph. 4:13).[12] Paul's warnings are not just for the individual, but he constantly stresses the effect of sin on the church and her ability to testify to the truth of Jesus Christ.

One would think that due to the devastating nature of sin on ourselves and on our community, we would take every precaution against it. However, the opposite appears to be true. Christians fully

---

11. Cornelius Plantinga, *Not the Way It's Supposed to Be: A Breviary of Sin* (Grand Rapids: Eerdmans, 1995), 32.

12. Compare 1 Corinthians 14:20: "Brothers, do not be children in your thinking. Be infants in evil, but in your thinking be mature."

immerse themselves in the secular bath of ideology and materialism. I frequently survey the groups to which I speak on what percentage of their average day they spend learning and reflecting on biblical truth, versus how much time they spend on activities that plunge them into the secular culture. The results are typically that less than 1–5 percent of an average day consists of combating the false ideas that come into our already depraved minds. Women in our churches are drowning in a sea of secular influence due to all sorts of activities and commitments that are not necessarily bad in and of themselves; yet, they are completely missing out on what truly matters. As a result, we spiral downward in the pursuit of what we think will bring us happiness—pleasure—instead of pursuing the knowledge which can truly heal and truly bring a biblical sense of happiness and human flourishing. We allow the peace of Christ found in renewing the mind to evade us and evade our relationships with one another.

In one of his smaller works, Francis Schaeffer, one of the twentieth century's greatest apologists, discusses how our unity and love will affect others around us. In *The Mark of a Christian*, the late Schaeffer refers to the "final apologetic" of Jesus, an apology based in the unity of the believers and their demonstrated love for one another. Love is an interesting argument to use as an apologetic defense. Very few people seem truly comfortable with the idea that real love, as a free choice, does not actually exist. Even atheist author and cognitive scientist Daniel Dennett states, " I would not want to live in a world without love. . . . I surmise that we almost all want a world in which love, justice, freedom, and peace are all present, as much as possible, but if we had to give up one of these, it wouldn't—and shouldn't—be love."[13] Even though Dennett is a Darwinian fundamentalist (and therefore must reduce "love" to something like reproductive and survival instincts), his view of love here suggests that he cannot fully do away with what we instinctively think of as love: a free choice of a human's will.

Love is a powerful medium through which to communicate.

---

13. Daniel C. Dennett, *Breaking the Spell: Religion as a Natural Phenomenon* (New York: Penguin, 2007), 254.

Schaeffer saw this power in Jesus' prayer for His followers in John 17:13–26. Of this passage, Schaeffer remarks,

> Now comes the sobering part. Jesus goes on in this 21st verse to say something that always causes me to cringe. If as Christians we do not cringe, it seems to me we are not very sensitive or very honest, because Jesus here gives us the final apologetic. What is the final apologetic? "That all of them may be one, Father, just as you are in me and I am in you. May they also be in us so that the world may believe that you have sent me." This is the final apologetic. . . . Here Jesus is stating something else which is much more cutting, much more profound: we cannot expect the world to believe that the Father sent the Son, that Jesus' claims are true, and that Christianity is true, unless the world sees some reality of the oneness of true Christians. Now that is frightening.[14]

According to Jesus, if the world does not see the love that true Christians have for one another, it will not believe that He was sent by God, that His claims are true, or that Christianity is true. This is a sobering thought when we consider how Christians consistently treat one another in the church today. Jesus basically lays out the evangelism bomb by connecting the oneness of the body of Christ as observed by the world with their discernment that Jesus was the Son of God (vv. 21, 23). What a great reminder for those who are engaged in outreach programs but fail to demonstrate unity and love toward the Christians with whom they are working. Evangelism begins in your heart with love toward your brother or sister in Christ. This love is noticed by the people in the world who then desire to

---

14. Francis Schaeffer, "The Mark of a Christian," in *The Complete Works of Francis A. Schaeffer: A Christian Worldview*, vol. 4, (Wheaton, IL: Crossway, 1982), 189.

know the reason for the love you have for one another. As the North African church father Tertullian stated about the view of Christians by non-Christians, "But it is mainly the deeds of a love so noble that lead many to put a brand upon us. *See*, they say, *how they love one another.*"[15] It is through our actions toward others that we not only show our true beliefs about God, but our interaction within the body of Christ is also a testimony to the validity of Jesus Christ as God's Son.

HOW OTHERS PERCEIVE OUR FAITH

As we go about our daily actions, other people notice *what* we do and *how* we do it. Since our actions are motivated by our beliefs, observers of our daily choices and actions are really seeing and, more importantly, analyzing, our beliefs. A number of women have told me that their families act one way at church and then completely change once they are outside church doors. What beliefs do these actions communicate? Certainly, in such situations there is a compartmentalization between what is professed and what is truly believed. In a worst case scenario, we might convey that we do not really believe what we profess. Consider when we discuss the sacrificial love of Jesus at church; do we act out of that belief as soon as we hit the pavement?

Perhaps those most affected by our beliefs are our children. Although we intuitively know that parents pass along their beliefs to their children, research over the past forty years has also confirmed this. The influence of a mother in the religious development and socialization of her children is great. In a 2008 study of the *Transmission of Religious Beliefs in College Students*, researchers state, "Mothers have been found to be more influential than fathers on the frequency of the overt religious behavior and church attendance of their children (Francis & Gibson, 1993)."[16] This research highlights a general trend

15. Alexander Roberts, James Donaldson, and Arthur Cleveland Cox, *The Ante-Nicene Fathers Vol. III: Translations of the Writings of the Fathers Down to A.D. 325*, Latin Christian: Its Founder, Tertullian, electronic edition of the Edinburgh ed. (Oak Harbor: Logos Research Systems, 1997), 46.

16. Ilana M. Milevsky, Lenore Szuchman, and Avidan Milevsky, "Transmission of

on the impact of a mother's beliefs on her children. The results of a 2003 study on parent-child communication about religion provide "direct evidence of mothers' major role, through dialogue with their children, in children's religious socialization."[17]

I do not intend to convey that a mother's influence is more important than a father's influence. In at least one of the studies, a father's religious attendance and activities were greater predictors of the child's religious attendance and activities; this was true to an even greater extent with daughters.[18] Further, agreement between the parents on beliefs and practices creates an even greater positive impact on children's beliefs than either parent alone. However, my focus is on women. We must understand how important a mother's *demonstrated* beliefs and values are in the development of her children's views. An article from the *Journal of Marriage and Family* provides additional support for the idea that much of what a child learns is based on day-to-day observation of attitudes and behavior performed by role models, such as parents.[19] Basically, a mother's beliefs as demonstrated through her attitude and actions, will influence what her children

---

Religious Beliefs in College Students," *Mental Health, Religion & Culture* 11, no. 4 (May 2008), 423–34.

17. Chris J. Boyatzis and Denise L. Janicki, "Parent-Child Communication about Religion: Survey and Diary Data on Unilateral Transmission and Bi-Directional Reciprocity Styles," Religious and Spiritual Development: Special Issue, *Review of Religious Research* 44, no. 3, (March 2003), 265. See also Roger L. Dudley and Margaret G. Dudley, "Transmission of Religious Values from Parents to Adolescents," *Review of Religious Research* 28, no. 1 (September 1986), 13. This article supports findings from earlier studies such as Acock & Bengtson (1978), as well as Newcomb & Svehla (1937).

18. Dianne K. Kieren and Brenda Munro, "RESEARCH NOTE: Following the Leaders: Parents' Influence on Adolescent Religious Activity," *Journal for the Scientific Study of Religion* 26, no. 2 (June 1987), 249–55. There seems to be some control factors for the studies that give different, even somewhat contradictory, results. The overall trend, though, is that maternal beliefs are a greater predictor of a child's beliefs.

19. Bao Wan-Ning et al., "Perceived Parental Acceptance as a Moderator of Religious Transmission Among Adolescent Boys and Girls," *Journal of Marriage and Family* 61, no. 2, (May 1999), 362–74.

ultimately believe is true about the world, especially with regard to the truth about God. If a mother does not value religious education and reasoning of her beliefs, her attitude will likely manifest itself in her daily actions and be transmitted to her children.

However, not all women are mothers or even will be mothers. So what about the rest of our sphere of influence? One of the major concerns being voiced by ladies attending my sessions is that they do not know how to broach the subject of God with those who are not believers in God or who have backgrounds in different religions. They greatly desire to talk with these folks about belief in God, but feel intimidated and unprepared. One of the things I point out first is that we are putting too much burden on ourselves to handle every single question that comes our way (addressed more in chapter 4). However, then I emphasize the necessity to be able to see a thoughtful person who is serious about her own belief (or disbelief) in God. In my interaction with atheists, in particular, I have heard over and over stories of Christians who could not answer even basic questions about their belief in God and how negatively this affected the atheist. Even sitting in on a church discipleship course on apologetics, I experienced an interaction between an atheist who knew the writings of the early church fathers on the subject matter being taught better than the Christian teacher of the course. Instead of admitting he did not know the teaching of early church father Augustine, the Christian teacher evaded the atheist's questioning and concern. What kind of belief are we modeling for the world if we cannot be honest about our own education?

In his book *Why I Believed,* atheist author and former missionary Kenneth W. Daniels made a case against the apathy of evangelical Christians toward learning about their beliefs and how this apathy adversely affected his own trust in God:

> In all my years of faithful church attendance, Bible studies, Christian college, missions training, and seminary, I do not recall one sermon, not one injunction encouraging me to examine my faith critically. Imagine your pastor preaching this from the

pulpit next Sunday: "I believe the Christian faith is true. As such, it can withstand any criticism. I encourage you not to take my word that it is true, nor the Bible's word, nor C. S. Lewis' word, nor anyone else's word. Think for yourself and come to your own conclusions. Probe your faith mercilessly to see whether it can stand the test."[20]

Notice that Daniels was looking for a specific type of encouragement within the church community. He wanted someone to challenge him to investigate why he believes what he believes. Though I do not agree with many of Daniels's conclusions and I found that his inquiries have been reasonably and thoughtfully answered by modern scholarship, I think we can take away a great lesson from him.

People notice our commitment to truth; that is, whether or not this commitment is present in our lives. We will model our commitment to the truth about God much better when we make the commitment a reality in our own lives. If we are not willing to sacrifice for gaining truth, it will show up in our interaction with others. The book of Proverbs warns believers to love wisdom above all else, because nothing can compare with wisdom (3:13–15). The New International Version of the Bible translates Proverbs 4:7, "The beginning of wisdom is this: Get wisdom. Though it cost all you have, get understanding." Yet, I can say that this will be one of the most challenging efforts of our lives.

From my experience, atheists and others notice when we lack commitment to the truth and lack seriousness about our beliefs. I meet these folks every month, and while I do not have a statistic to quote, I can tell you each one has a story about a Christian or a church. I know there are some logical problems with equating an individual's belief or absence of belief in God with the actions of fallen human beings in the church. Yet, because there is an effect of our

20. Kenneth W. Daniels, "Why I Believed: Reflections of a Former Missionary," *The Secular Web.* http://www.infidels.org/library/modern/ken_daniels/why.html.

beliefs on those around us, we should take a look at where our ministries are focused and how our individual members are perceived in their community. Do people see the women in your church as serious members of a faith community who are willing to tackle the difficult questions that arise? Do they see Christian women who are willing to discover the truth about this life, wherever the truth may lead? Our communities are watching us and the beliefs they see lived out will impact their lives.

Jesus not only told us to engage our communities, but He gave us the immense task of making an impact for Him in the world around us. Our discipling extends to all people of all nations; we are called to discover where individuals are on their path to discovering truth and then to meet them there. Sometimes, this will mean answering difficult questions. Sometimes, it will involve just being available for someone who is hurting. Other times, it will be a mix of things. The women's ministry is a perfect place to begin maturing the body of Christ, so that our ladies will be ones who step up to the challenge of ministering truth in a fallen world.

The first three chapters of this book are meant to aid the development of effective women's ministries through focusing on the belief of individuals. As the individual believer becomes transformed, so goes the transformation of the women's ministry. Although I didn't propose any groundbreaking new material, I've sought to awaken those ideas which may have been latent in our minds. If our women's ministries are going to effectively engage their culture, they need women who know why they believe, understand how their beliefs affect them personally, and are conscientious that those beliefs will affect their communities.

Chapter 4

WHAT YOU CAN DO RIGHT NOW

*I never thought to ask a person questions about
what they believed. I was taught just to tell people
what I believed. It makes sense to find out where they
are at in life and start from there.*
—Women's conference attendee

Some of my most precious memories are captured in catch phrases my parents used to impart little gems of wisdom. My mom used to say, "People will judge you by the friends you keep," and "You should give to those who are less fortunate than you and be thankful for what you have." My dad had a different type of wisdom to impart. He used to say, "Don't do anything stupid," which was later followed with "I think you out-stupid-ed yourself," when I did do something stupid.

I had a good laugh the other day remembering Dad's wisdom as I came across a blog entry entitled "How to convert atheists."[1] One of the author's first pieces of advice was "Don't be stupid." Since the wisdom so closely aligned with that of my father, I read on and found a refreshing bit of honesty about how Christians should interact with atheists if they want to be taken seriously. A few of author's points

---

1. Luke Muehlhauser, "How to Convert Atheists," *Common Sense Atheism*, last modified August 13, 2009. http://commonsenseatheism.com/?p=2090.

would be a great place to start our investigation of how to interact with others about our belief in God.

First of all, and most importantly, be realistic. Most people are already too entrenched in what they believe to convert to your beliefs on the spot, so whether you are street witnessing or just talking to a family member, do not expect someone to be interested right away. There's no need to get uptight or anxious about your conversation or worry about how the other person responds because you are probably just going to have a quick conversation on your differing viewpoints. Also remember that sometimes the purpose for engaging others is just to help other people think well, too. You should care about the education of our human community.

Secondly, you need to seek to explore the truth with people. We are coming out of an era of Christian culture in which we have been taught, "The Bible says it, I believe it, that settles it." There is a sense in which this statement is true: God's special revelation is the ultimate truth on what it teaches. However, an underlying message is that Christians are not open to discussion on belief in God. This message comes across loud and clear to those who are not followers of Jesus, and today when we try discussing belief in God with others, we have to combat the image this message has conveyed over the years. If people who do not believe are to trust you with a conversation about God, they need to know you are open to discovering the truth, no matter where it may lead.

Finally, the author of the blog strongly urges Christians to come prepared. Christians should actually study "philosophy of religion, historical method, epistemology, and so on. Study the arguments for God and present the best ones in their strongest form. Study popular atheistic arguments and be prepared to give solid—not evasive—answers to them."[2] He cites 1 Peter 3:15, saying that Christians are always to be prepared to give an answer for the reason of the hope that is within them. I wholeheartedly agree with him on this point.

In reality, however, many Christians are just not at this point of in-depth study yet; come to think of it, neither are many atheists or

---

2. Ibid.

agnostics.[3] In the rest of this chapter, I will present a good place for all of us to start, with an obvious emphasis on Christians. We will consider four actions to help us step into a public faith that takes responsibility for what we believe. My hope is that Christians will live out what we profess because we understand it and truly believe it. Also, I hope we will once again become a culture that influences the whole of humanity, publicly and boldly spreading truth and light from an honest and confident belief in God.

Action #1: Know

The first action Christians should take toward stepping into a public faith is to know what they believe. As we step out into the world proclaiming that we have the answers to the problems of humankind, we must have a good working knowledge of those answers. This is part of being a good representative or ambassador for Christ. In his book *Tactics: A Game Plan for Discussing Your Christian Convictions,* Greg Koukl notes that the first skill of a good ambassador is knowledge.[4] The United States only sends out people who are knowledgeable in U.S. foreign policy to be ambassadors from our nation to another nation. In Christianity, we are all ambassadors sent out by the Lord Jesus Christ and should do our best to accurately represent His "policies."

One area of basic importance is the knowledge of essential Christian doctrines. These beliefs identify a person as "Christian," versus identifying her with other religious or non-religious adherences. I call these the non-negotiables of the Christian faith. Some of these include the following:

- God's unity and triunity

- Christ's deity and humanity

---

3. These observations are based in my experiences, not on statistical research.
4. Greg Koukl, *Tactics: A Game Plan for Discussing Your Christian Convictions* (Grand Rapids: Zondervan, 2009), 25.

- The virgin birth

- Christ's sinlessness

- Christ's atoning death, bodily resurrection, and bodily ascension

- Human depravity

- The necessity of grace and faith

- Christ's priestly intercession

- Christ's bodily second coming

- The inerrancy of Scripture[5]

This is not an exhaustive list but serves to introduce the concepts and hopefully to encourage you to study why you personally hold each doctrine to be true (or to discover if you do hold them to be true). When we stray from any one of these doctrines, we are no longer professing the basic orthodox Christianity which has united us as a faith across time and denominations. In fact, many of the early heresies in the church were based in the first few doctrines, usually in reference to the person of Jesus. Some said Jesus was God's Son, but He was completely emptied of His divinity; He was only a human son of God. Others failed to recognize Jesus as the Son of God at all. In 2 Corinthians 11, Paul warns the Corinthians against people in the church who preached a different Jesus than the one he had originally preached to them. He also warns the Galatians that they should not accept an alternative gospel even if Paul himself or an angel preached it (Gal. 1:6–8). These warnings hold true today. In order to keep from following after false

---

5. Adapted from Norman Geisler and Ron Rhodes, *Conviction Without Compromise: Standing Strong in the Core Beliefs of the Christian Faith* (Eugene, OR: Harvest House, 2008), 3.

teaching, and thus being poor ambassadors, we need to take personal responsibility for our religious doctrines.[6] We also need to take personal responsibility for our knowledge of God Himself.

Another area of focus in Christian doctrine are the attributes of God. Bible studies often focus on one attribute, such as God's love for us or His sovereignty over the world. However, as part of His perfection, God completely holds all attributes equally and at the same time. This is an important piece of the puzzle as we strive to understand difficult issues like the problem of evil, the mercy and love of God, and real justice.[7] If we focus solely on God's love, we can be at a loss to understand His judgment. If we just learn of God's justice, we can encounter difficulty comprehending His mercy and forgiveness. Failure to educate our congregations on the full spectrum of God's attributes has allowed many who take issue with one aspect of God without understanding the other aspects, to drift away. To be honest in our conversations, we have to take the fullness of the Christian view of God, not just one aspect we want to support or attack. Oprah Winfrey demonstrated this problem in her religious Internet course, *A New Earth*. In the first episode, she told a caller that she could not comprehend following a jealous God, because a God that was jealous of her didn't feel right in her spirit. So she ended up leaving the church. Oprah left the traditional Christian faith because she had a problem with one characteristic of God, erroneously isolated from

---

6. See "Suggested Resources" for recommended readings on these doctrines.

7. Problem of evil questions center around how an all-good or all-loving God who is all powerful and all knowing could allow instances of evil and suffering when He is willing and able to do otherwise. The conclusion made by skeptics is that this kind of God must not exist. Long time Christian philosophers, Alvin Plantinga (*God, Freedom, and Evil* [Grand Rapids: Eerdmans, 1974]), Paul Copan (http://www.paulcopan.com), and William Lane Craig (http://www.reasonablefaith.com) as well as up-and-coming philosopher David Wood ("Responding to the Argument from Evil," and "God, Suffering and Santa Claus," in William A. Dembski and Michael C. Licona, eds., *Evidence for God* [Grand Rapids: Baker Books, 2010]) extensively address the problem of evil. Visit http://www.apologetics315.com to find links to each philosopher's material.

the rest of His characteristics. I have found that if I am to have a productive conversation about God with someone, I must try to correct their similar misconceptions of the Christian view of God.

One way that I have tried to clear up misconceptions is by asking people what God must be like in order to be worthy of the title "God." In a conversation with an atheist friend about God's attributes, I asked, "If God exists, what would He have to be like in order to be called 'God'?" My friend responded with a long list of characteristics to consider (not just one or a few, as in the example of Oprah's rejection of God). His list basically mirrored the Christian view of God's attributes. So I asked him, "Why aren't you a Christian? Because you've just listed the attributes of the Christian God!" Though I was partially teasing my friend for upholding a Christian view of God while professing atheism, I desired for him to discover a fuller comprehension of the nature of God. From his own understanding came a list that included perfectly just, loving, good, forgiving, and merciful, as well as eternally existing and the first cause of the universe. His view of God's nature was similar to my own—though not exactly the same. He gave me a great jumping off point for conversation! Had I not asked him about his view of "God," I wouldn't have been able to point out important differences.

Realistically, there are going to be some (many!) things about God that we will not know because we are His creation and He is not ours. However, since we can know what has been revealed to us through reason, evidence, and the witness of the Holy Spirit, we should use all available information in assessing our view of God and in responsibly presenting the Christian God to others. Knowing the attributes of the God we profess aids our understanding of the various views of God and is invaluable for conversation with people of differing views. How can we profess the good news of God if we do not know the God of the good news? Again, an important part of being a good ambassador for God is to know His essential characteristics, that is, His attributes.[8]

---

8. See "Suggested Resources" for recommended books that address the attributes of God.

As Christians gain knowledge about their beliefs, they can gain confidence that their beliefs are true. In John 14:6, Jesus states, "I am the way, and the truth, and the life. No one comes to the Father except through me." Jesus is responding to a disciple's question of how he will find the way to Jesus once Jesus has gone to "his Father's house." Jesus tells him that the disciples know the way because He is the way; meaning the way to God. He qualifies His statement by saying He is the truth and the life. Jesus here does not say He is teaching the way or He is pointing out the way, but rather that He is the actual way to God. He is the embodiment of God, who is truth and life. So Jesus is also making an objective claim that He is the embodiment of truth.

As evangelical Christians, we believe that since He is God, Jesus is actually the truth. He is the Divine Logos who created all things at the beginning of time, including all truth. According to Colossians 1:15–17, "He is the image of the invisible God, the firstborn of all creation. For by him all things were created, in heaven and on earth, visible and invisible, whether thrones or dominions or rulers or authorities—all things were created through him and for him. And he is before all things, and in him all things hold together." So when Christians speak about their belief in God, they are speaking about actual truth, not just something that's nice for them or that makes for a good story.[9] If you are going to say "I'm a Christian," this entails beliefs such as those found in Colossians 1 and in John 14:6—Jesus Christ as truth personified—and you should have knowledge that what you say is true. As Christian philosopher William Lane Craig explained, "The Christian, therefore, can never look on the truth with apathy or disdain. Rather, he cherishes and treasures the truth as a reflection of God Himself."[10] It is also intellectually dishonest to tell people you believe you have the truth, when you do not know what

---

9. There are differences of opinion among those who self-identify as "Christian" within Western culture. My main audience in this book is evangelical Christians.

10. William Lane Craig, "In Intellectual Neutral" in *Passionate Conviction*, ed. William Lane Craig and Paul Copan (Nashville, TN: Broadman & Holman, 2007), 4.

that truth entails or why you believe it. For me, knowledge of basic doctrines and reasons for why you believe in God are a bare minimum requirement for believers in God. Of course, I am not saying that this list is required knowledge for salvation. Nor am I suggesting that anyone needs to achieve a certain level of academic work before they can speak about their faith. To be clear, I am saying if you are going to profess what you believe is the absolute truth about this world, you should be able to articulate the beliefs that you profess. Another reason we need to do this is specifically for the purpose of fulfilling the Great Commission.

In Matthew 28:19–20, Jesus tells His disciples, "Go therefore and make disciples of all nations, baptizing them in the name of the Father and of the Son and of the Holy Spirit, teaching them to observe all that I have commanded you." However, there have been studies and surveys over the last twenty years demonstrating that proportionally few Christians are engaging in the Great Commission.[11] In fact, the statistics probably mirror what many of us know to be true in our own lives and communities. Many Christian women do not engage non-Christians in conversations about God, even though they are able to discuss nearly any other issue. This is because Christians may struggle with a few issues internally. First, one may lack confidence in what she believes either due to doubt, a lack of knowledge, or a lack of commitment to the truth. Second, one may be fearful of the unknown. One way to cure the fear is to face it: start talking to people. Though I have been told I am very outgoing, I have those moments in which I must remind myself that it is okay to talk with others about religious views. In fact, many of my most interesting conversations have entailed meeting new people and discussing their beliefs.

Finally, the Christian woman is probably putting too much burden on herself for having all the answers. While most of what has been written so far has centered on knowing reasons for your own Christian beliefs, the Christian is not the only one with a set of beliefs to explain. Other people have beliefs, too. One important aspect of

---

11. The Pew Forum on Religion and the Barna Research Group engage in such research.

dialog with our communities is to find out why others profess the beliefs they hold, and to interact with those explanations. In the words of my dad, if you do not hold others accountable for knowledge of their beliefs, you are "out-stupid-ing" yourself.

Action #2: Listen

I am not the best listener. I have an annoying tendency to break into a person's explanation or story to interact with it, or worse, to relate it back to something about me. Being married to a man who is as gracious as he is astute has helped me mature in this area. He has a kind way of helping me in conversations by directing the attention toward others, hoping that I pick up on his cue and come along. Over the years, I have learned to pick up his lead and have even asked him later how he perceived conversations in which I felt I may have been overbearing. As I slowly become a better listener, a world of learning opportunities opens up. Being a better listener has also vastly improved my interactions in apologetics. People are much more interested in interacting with me because I will listen intently to their views.

People usually know when you are not really listening to them or when you are not interested in the conversation. If you want to display a Christian faith that values sincerity, then you must develop a genuine interest in other people and their views as you interact with them. This entails truly hearing them, not just latching onto one point and formulating an argument while they are still talking. Proverbs 18:13 says, "If anyone gives an answer before he hears, it is his folly and shame." I have been too quick to judge in the past because I did not listen to a person's full argument before making an assessment. Further, I forget what the other person's points were because I too quickly stop listening, stifling any fuller comprehension. To remedy this situation, I repeat the main points and ask if I correctly understand them. Repeating a person's points back to him or her will not only help you understand the points, but it will help you form better arguments. Good communication is vital to the task of sharing our beliefs and discussing truth. It should not be a secondary endeavor, but one of primacy. I have seen highly intelligent, knowledgeable Christians lose the interest and respect of another woman because they fail to convey a true interest in her and in her view. Since engaging in apologetics with non-Christians is ultimately part of evangelism, our conversations should be entered into with all the respect due the person with whom we want to share Christ.

If you find repeating arguments does not help you remember or understand, perhaps you could write down the main points and ask for clarification on the ones that are troublesome. I frequently do this when I am giving a presentation. It might look a bit awkward, but appearances can take a hit for the sake of truly understanding an issue. Keep a small notepad in your purse, in the car, or at your desk. I usually travel with a spiral bound notebook if I think I am going to be asked difficult questions. I have never been sorry for writing down a question to help aid my memory. Quite to the contrary, I find it extremely helpful in demonstrating my desire to thoughtfully interact with the audience or with the person right in front of me.

WHAT YOU WILL DISCOVER

On a flight from Los Angeles to Dallas, I was seated next to a man who, during the preliminary checks and announcements, talked very quietly on a cell phone, with his hand cupped over the entire phone and his body curled up toward the wall. It seemed pretty clear that he wanted nothing to do with me or anyone else. So I opened up Dallas Willard's book *The Divine Conspiracy* and began to read. Shortly thereafter, he finished his conversation, settled into his seat, and un-expectedly took a gander at my book's title. He said, "That looks like an interesting read. What is the book about?"[12] Since I had already prepared myself for a disinterested or even sleeping seatmate, I wasn't ready to give a coherent response. I managed to say something like, "There's a conspiracy going on . . . God's after you and He wants you

---

12. When I read Christian books with catchy titles on airplane trips, I am frequently asked questions about the content of the books. If you are not a particularly good conversation starter, a conversation piece such as a book might be a helpful way to pique someone's interest.

for Himself!" After my somewhat embarrassing and vague explanation, an exciting conversation ensued.

The gentleman, I learned, was a practicing Buddhist. I was very interested to find out what exactly he believed and why he had chosen Buddhism. As he described his Buddhist beliefs, he stated that there is no right or wrong, good or evil, there just *is*. The way things are is the ways things are. I made a mental note of this major philosophical difference between Buddhism and Christianity. As we continued our lively conversation, I asked him many questions about himself and his religious life. We eventually came to the subject of politics, and he adamantly insisted that the American involvement in Iraq was wrong. I asked him, "You said earlier that there is no right or wrong according to Buddhist beliefs. How does a Buddhist reconcile that view with the belief that the war in Iraq is wrong?" He stopped and thought for a long moment, and it was clear that he had never been asked this kind of question before. He said, "I guess I'm still working out my selfish desires," a response that came out of his Buddhist beliefs as well. I hope he saw from my question that his particular view of the world is impossible to live out, because we all make choices every day based on what we believe is right or wrong. Even his own choice to be Buddhist is based on the idea that Buddhism was the right choice concerning religious beliefs; otherwise, why would he choose anything at all? Because I listened carefully and really tried to learn about what he believed, I was able to engage him on his ideology.

There are two general discoveries you will make when you listen to people discuss belief in God. First, many people have not really thought about belief in God, and second, you can find much to discuss when you really hear what others are saying. Most people, even religious folks, do not give much time to learning about their beliefs about God. A recent Barna poll shows that we live in one of the most theologically illiterate periods in history.[13] One of the great Christian traditions has been to promote literacy and education wherever we have gone. The time is ripe for a reminder and return to this grand

---

13. "Six Megathemes Emerge from Barna Group Research in 2010," The Barna Group, last modified December 13, 2010, http://www.barna.org/culture-articles/462-six-megathemes-emerge-from-2010.

tradition. Of course, we have to start with ourselves, but then we need to listen to others to see how we can help create a renaissance of reasoned belief. You will find there is much disbelief that is irresponsible and based in emotion or in hearsay. This kind of disbelief does not involve an open and honest personal investigation. Part of our testimony to the truth is to point out when we see poor reasoning. Helping our community reason better is part of loving our neighbor. Our responsibility to love our neighbor as ourselves does not merely involve politeness, but it also includes a concern for each other's understanding and comprehension of the world in which we live. I say this with no smugness, but with a teacher's heart. One way I love people is by helping them discover truth. I cannot do so without listening to them and to what they believe is true.

Many Christians worry about what they will say to certain questions or how they will respond to certain accusations. In the next section, we will discuss some conversational questions for interactive purposes, but generally you will find what you can discuss by paying attention to what people say. Many of us are way too defensive when we hear something that goes against our own belief in God. We get a rush of anger or adrenaline, and we want to hide somewhere, hurt someone, or at least make sure we get to play the trump card. When this happens, emotions are in control and we usually do not hear what is actually being said. If you will let that wave of emotion pass and then go back through the person's statement or points, you will most likely find some things you can open up for discussion. We need to be quick to hear, slow to speak, slow to anger, for "the anger of man does not produce the righteousness of God" (James 1:19–20). Instead of just being defensive about things we hear, we can find paths to discovering truth along with the person standing in front of us (or at the other end of the e-mail, text message, Facebook post, etc.).

Dietrich Bonhoeffer was a brilliant Christian thinker and an outspoken opponent of the Nazi regime in Germany. He wrote a work called *Life Together* during his time as a seminary teacher in an underground church network in Nazi Germany. In a section entitled "Service," Bonhoeffer describes the importance God ascribes to listening: "It is God's love for us that He not only gives us His Word but also lends us His ear. So it is His work that we do for our brother when we learn to listen to him."[14] A Christian usually thinks that their gift to others is to offer something, such as a response, but sometimes our gift is to listen. The atheist, Muslim, Hindu, and Mormon are our brothers and sisters in God's creation. We have the opportunity to share God's love for man through listening, but we can also show that we respect the person by asking for a reasoning of their beliefs. Holding a person accountable for reasonable views means that you think they are the kind of person who is responsible and capable of discerning and understanding truth.

Action #3: Question

In 2008, Greg Koukl of Stand to Reason ministries jokingly introduced me on his radio program as a "strange bird." He said I was strange because I was one of comparatively few women Christian apologists at the time. However, my methods of discussion are not strange and are not unlike Koukl's methods. We both think you should ask people a lot of questions about what they believe instead of jumping into long-winded explanations of doctrines and evidences. We find Jesus Himself asking people a lot of questions during His ministry. He frequently responded to a question with a question or He gave a question in return after His answer. Many of these instances involved highly intelligent people, such as the Pharisees or Sadducees, who were trying to entrap Jesus in a logical problem with the law.[15] We would do well to follow Jesus' example, even when it involves people who very well may be smarter than we are. By asking questions, we are able to discover where people are in their beliefs. A basic approach

---

14. Dietrich Bonhoeffer, *Life Together: A Discussion of Christian Fellowship* (New York: Harper and Row, 1954), 97.

15. A few of these instances can be found back-to-back in Matthew 22: the question of the lawfulness of paying taxes; the question of the seven brothers who married the same widow and the resurrection; and the question of the greatest commandment.

is to use the old interrogative questions we learned back in grade school: Who? What? Where? When? Why? How?

One of the first questions I ask when someone makes a statement or asks a question about Christianity is "What do you mean by that?"[16] This question became a staple in my repertoire after several occasions of answering questions people were not asking and assuming what people did not intend. When I ask this question, the person making the statement gets a chance to clarify and refine their position, question, or statement. The further explanation helps guide our conversations toward a more productive and efficient end. We actually answer what they are really asking! How many times have you encountered a situation where a person misunderstood what you said and your intention in saying it? Wouldn't you have liked someone to ask you a clarifying question?

A second benefit of asking "What do you mean by that?" is that I get the "author's intent." Back in elementary school, as part of learning about how to approach understanding a story, we learned to keep in mind the author's intent. What was the author's purpose in writing the material? Was the author trying to persuade, inform, or entertain? By asking people what they mean, we can also get at their purpose for making a statement or for asking a question about the Christian faith. Sometimes, an individual's intention is not so nice, and our question is a way of graciously engaging a person who may have originally meant harm, yet finds us undaunted by malicious intent.

The next question in the series of interrogative questions is "Why do you believe that?" This question helps you discover things you can discuss. Here's where you will begin to see a person's reasons for rejecting belief in God. You are then able to interact with those specific reasons. After thoroughly addressing one issue, you can move to the other reasons as the situation allows. I recommend staying on one issue until it has been fully treated to the best of your knowledge. Quick changes in the subject do not help you and your conversation

---

16. Koukl also uses this question as part of his interaction with others. He has a great way of teaching the questions through the use of the "Columbo" method, based on the old Columbo television series.

partner discover what is true. This is generally true across our spectrum of knowledge; when we really want to learn something we dig deep into the issue and stay there awhile. You can frame the "why" question in different ways:

- Why do you think that is true?

- Why do you find that to be the case?

- Why don't you believe in God?

The third question I like to use is "How do you know that?" In the "why" series of questions, we are trying to understand a person's reasoning for a belief. In the "how" series, we want to know the evidence used to arrive at the belief. These two questions can elicit similar answers. However, it is useful to consider them separately because the why is not always associated with the how in answering for a person's beliefs. A "why" can be answered with an emotional commitment, such as "because it felt so good." This response was given to me in another airplane conversation when I asked a lady why she believed she had met God three times. Apparently, the woman's heart had flat-lined three separate times in her life and each time she was convinced she met God. When I asked, "Why do you believe that," she replied, "Because it felt so good." The next question I asked was "How do you know it was God and not something else?" She understood this to mean I wanted evidence or some knowledge external to her feelings. She was not able to provide any external evidence that could validate that her feelings had given her true knowledge about God. I told her that this would pose a problem for me. In other areas of my life I want to know what is true, not just what I feel. My feelings about situations have been completely wrong before and I needed to accept correction. Since the area of knowledge dealing with God is the most important area—due to the implications on our lives—I would want to be more certain than what my emotions or feelings alone could provide. This is the reason for asking the "how" questions: to keep in check the emotional side of belief. As the prophet Jeremiah wrote,

"The heart is deceitful above all things, and desperately sick; who can understand it?" (Jer. 17:9). Some of the other "how" questions include the following:

- How did you come to that understanding about (God, religion, social issue, etc.)?

- How do you know that is the truth?

- How have you come to this conclusion?

This last question, "How have you come to this conclusion?" is an important question to ask. Not many people have spent quality time searching for an answer to the question of belief in God. If people are going to adamantly hold to a position, it is responsible of them to know how they came to their conclusion. Did they research both sides of the arguments and grapple with the issues involved? Did they spend much time in reflection, honestly considering each part of the argument? What opposing arguments were the most difficult to reconcile with their current position? J. P. Moreland and Klaus Issler follow the same line of questioning in their book *In Search of a Confident Faith*. When Moreland encounters challenges to the Christian faith presented by a person, he states, "I'm sure you have formulated your viewpoint against Christianity in a fair-minded and intellectually responsible way by studying *both* sides of the issue. Since this is so, tell me, what were the four to five best books you have read that *defend* the Christian answer to your claim? And what were the three or four best arguments *against* your conclusion that you had to address in arriving at your skeptical stance, and how did you answer these arguments?"[17]

Finally, the last three interrogative questions include who, where, and when? Though you will not use all questions in every

---

17. J. P. Moreland and Klaus Issler, *In Search of a Confident Faith: Overcoming Barriers to Trusting in God* (Downers Grove, IL: InterVarsity Press, 2008), 57.

conversation, these last few can serve as a reminder that we need to investigate beliefs to best of our ability before responding.

- Who is the author of this information?

- Who is the scientist/company behind that study?

- Whose philosophy are you using for your view?

- Where did you learn that?

- Where are you getting that from?

- When did you come to the point where you believed this was true?

Some of these questions just may not be your style or your way of saying things. I am a fairly direct person when it comes to discussing beliefs, so I tend to be a little more direct in my conversations. If you are a little less direct, Greg Koukl recommends a gentler way to introduce a question by saying, "Have you ever considered . . ." or "Can you help me understand this?" or "Can you clear this up for me?"[18] Most importantly, whatever you do and however you do it, make sure you are asking people questions. Asking questions is following the model of Jesus, who asked those who questioned Him to support their views.

In Matthew 22, a number of teachers approach Jesus in an attempt to knock down His reasoning and show Him to be a false prophet. More importantly, these teachers try to trap Jesus into saying something that would ultimately get Him arrested. After Jesus spoke harsh parables against the hypocrisy of the Pharisees and Sadducees, He is asked several questions (22:15–40). His answers astonished the

---

18. Koukl, *Tactics*, 84–85. See also Randy Newman, *Questioning Evangelism: Engaging People's Hearts the Way Jesus Did* (Grand Rapids: Kregel, 2004).

crowd. Twice Jesus asked a question in return to show that the religious leaders' views were not coherent.

One of these series of questions begins in verse 42, where Jesus asks, "What do you think about the Christ? Whose son is he?" The Pharisees answer, "The son of David" (v. 42). They have answered that the Messiah is just a man. Jesus then asks, "How is it then that David, in the Spirit, calls him Lord, saying 'The Lord said to my Lord, Sit at my right hand, until I put your enemies under your feet'" (vv. 43–44). The Pharisees have nothing to say in response. Jesus asks questions to help the Pharisees, and those listening, discover what it is they already know but are unwilling to say. The Pharisees would have known the passage Jesus quoted from Psalm 110, but they were unwilling to accept the Messiah as both God and man; they were unwilling to accept the implications of Jesus' true nature. Many times in conversations, we ask questions to help people see that their desires have outweighed what they know to be true. Jesus asked questions to undercover buried truth.

Perhaps you are not yet comfortable with simply asking questions. My encouragement to you is to practice. Does it sound odd that you would practice having a conversation? I know quite a few people who are not good conversationalists. They need to practice being a part of a conversation. Do what you need to do so that the next time someone rattles off a false or misleading comment about the Christian faith, you will automatically have a question to ask. Have a few questions ready to go at anytime in any situation. Conversing with people takes practice. As with anything worth doing, conversation about God is worth doing well. It's going to take some of your time and effort to be able to do so.

Action #4: Respond

The last step we need to take to make our faith public in an influential and meaningful way is to respond to statements and questions. If, in the course of a discussion, you find that the person does not have good evidence for a position or has made some statements that are incoherent or unlivable, point these things out. You don't have to do this in an unpleasant way. Remember my conversation with the Buddhist when I asked, "How does a Buddhist reconcile that view (that there is no right or wrong) with the belief that the war in Iraq is wrong?" Essentially, I was saying without being obnoxious that I didn't believe his was a livable philosophy. It is important to show people where they have faulty thinking in order to help them discover what is true. Sometimes we will not get all the way to the good news of Jesus Christ in one encounter, but our role may be to break up some of the poor reasoning that has been keeping them from investigating Jesus. The prophet Isaiah declared, "Truth has stumbled in the public squares, and uprightness cannot enter. Truth is lacking" (Isa. 59:14–15). This problem is still true today. And though we are mostly talking here about people who don't believe in God, the same problems can be found among some who say they do believe in God. There are irresponsible disbelievers and believers. Part of truly loving people is helping them discover the truth about this life, whatever their background.

Some questions you encounter will be valid questions. These questions usually result when people have spent some time thinking about an issue and it has stumped them or caused them to doubt the existence of God. The question I hear most frequently relates to the problem of evil: How can you say that God is good when there is so much evil, pain, and suffering in this world? This is an important question because it delves into the nature of God and into such ideas as "good" and "evil." When a person is struggling with a question such as this, it is our privilege to be able to respond. It also provides you with the opportunity to demonstrate integrity when you are unsure of an answer: "I don't know, but I will find out."

In *The Literal Meaning of Genesis* fourth-century scholar Saint Augustine noted:

> It is a disgraceful and dangerous thing for an infidel [unbeliever] to hear a Christian, presumably giving the meaning of Holy Scripture, talking nonsense on these topics [knowledge of the world]; and we should take all means to prevent such an

embarrassing situation in which people show up vast ignorance in a Christian and laugh it to scorn. . . . If they find a Christian mistaken in a field which they themselves know well, and hear him maintaining his foolish opinions about our books [Scriptures], how are they going to believe those books in matters concerning the resurrection of the dead, the hope of eternal life and the kingdom of heaven, when they think their pages are full of falsehoods on facts which they themselves have learnt from experience and the light of reason?[19]

Though Augustine specifically addressed Christians who interpreted Scripture according to their own view of a worldly issue, instead of accurately portraying the work of the biblical authors, his primary concern was for the integrity of the Christian witness. We must handle situations in which we are not knowledgeable with as much honesty and humility as we do an area in which we are skilled. As a representative of Jesus, the most powerful and intelligent being known to humankind, we should demonstrate that we are not shaken when we do not have all the answers. It is unreasonable to think that you can sincerely be knowledgeable on every question asked of you. However, as a follower of Christ—who is the way, the truth, and the life—the lack of an immediate answer should never throw you into despair. Instead, a question for which you have no answer is a chance for you to learn. You are only one person and you cannot possibly provide an answer to every single question.

Occasionally I am asked a question that is intended to make me look unintelligent or less intelligent than the person asking the question. Maybe you or the women in your ministry are fearful of the same thing. First, let us remember how ridiculous it is for anyone to put another person in this situation. There is much more knowledge

19. St. Augustine, *The Literal Meaning of Genesis*, trans. John Hammond Taylor, (New York: Paulist Press, 1982), book 1, chap. 19, http://college.holycross.edu/faculty/alaffey/other_files/Augustine-Genesis1.pdf.

available to learn in this world than any one individual will ever have time to comprehend. Specialization in a certain area of knowledge does not grant a person permission to be rude. A couple of questions that I use to respond are "Why do you think I should particularly know that (since I do not have a background in that area)?" and "What do you mean by that?" Another approach is to ask them to be the experts on the issues since they seem to be in the know.[20] This is a less confrontational approach than my first question above. If they are the experts, you can ask them to explain their views and the reasons to support it. You can then find some time to study a little in this area for your next interaction with the experts. Second, even if people seem to be arrogant, you can still learn from them. We don't have to let a person's attitude keep us from learning about a subject. Third, if the person represents a non-Christian view and wants to be persuasive toward that view, arrogance usually does more damage than good. A bad attitude turns the listener off to what could have been an interesting conversation.

Another situation that arises when discussing God with others is that some people will not answer questions or will not stay on a topic once you have responded to their initial comments. This is where you need to be discerning; don't spend large amounts of time with a person who is intellectually dishonest. Others should be answering your questions, listening to you when you speak, and interacting with your responses—just as you are. If people will not do these things, they are not honestly seeking to discover truth. Instead, they may just wish to antagonize and tear others down. I have encountered my fair share of these folks, and I usually answer them once or twice and then I move along to those who will stay on a subject and who aren't trying to attack me.[21] If you receive such attacks in the place of logically coherent arguments, your attacker demonstrates that they lack good arguments against your position. Take comfort from the

20. Koukl, *Tactics*, 68–70.
21. A personal attack like this is called an *Ad hominem* argument. It means to attack the person making an argument instead of the argument itself. Most of us are familiar with this from watching political advertisements.

Beatitudes, where Jesus says, "Blessed are you when others revile you and persecute you and utter all kinds of evil against you falsely on my account. Rejoice and be glad, for your reward is great in heaven, for so they persecuted the prophets who were before you" (Matt. 5:11–12). Keep in mind that most people you speak to at work, or at home, or out in public are not going to revile and persecute you. In fact, you will probably find them to be really interesting once you get the conversation started.

THE CONCLUSION OF THE MATTER

I never took true ownership for what I professed until I had my faith challenged by an opposing viewpoint. I went through a time of searching for answers to my own questions about the existence of God. During this search, I tried to be as unbiased as possible, yet it is nearly impossible to approach such an important issue as belief in God from a completely impartial position and with complete intellectual honesty. The famous philosopher, Rene Descartes, found such a task to be so difficult that he attempted to strip away everything he thought he knew and approach even the most basic knowledge, such as his own existence, from a standpoint of skepticism. Descartes used the example of a basket of apples to represent our ideas. He said you must examine every apple in the basket to see if there are any bad ones, because those few rotten apples could spoil the whole basket. Once examined, the good apples could then go back into the basket. I am not suggesting that we start from Descartes's level of skepticism: "How do I know I exist"? We can start with the question from Chapter 1, "Why do I believe in God?" When we find answers, we need to put our answers out into the public sphere.

> Typically, those who disagree with our ideas are better at keeping us honest than we are with ourselves. It is a more unbiased approach—than simply thinking you are being impartial—to consider the view of someone who completely disagrees with you on a matter. I am sure you can find a few folks with

opposing viewpoints who would love to tell you that you are wrong! This dialogue is so important to vibrant, personal faith in God: to be a public Christian who loves the truth over their own personal comfort. What do you do if you "out-stupid" yourself? Don't worry. People are mostly forgiving if you give them the opportunity. In addition, the Lord is always forgiving. Remember, it is not you that does the saving; it is always the Holy Spirit's work in the life of another person.

Chapter 5

WHAT YOU CAN DO IN WOMEN'S MINISTRY

*Why would a woman come to a session on
apologetics at a women's ministry conference?*
—Shirley Moses

We have established so far that to see real change in women's ministries, we need to get down to the root causes of why women in our churches remain unchanged. We have looked at the importance of being honest about our beliefs, the necessity of reasoning, the implications of our beliefs on our lives, and how women can get out into the world to test their beliefs with others by asking questions. While we certainly have not covered the entire spectrum of a Christian woman's life, all of these things will aid our ministries in transforming women. In this chapter, we will consider four practical goals for implementing apologetics studies into women's ministries.

GOAL #1: ESTABLISH THE NEED

Since apologetics is basically a new area for women's ministry, our first task is to help people understand the need. We want to emphasize the importance of having a ready defense of our Christian beliefs so we are able to talk with anyone who asks about our faith (1 Peter

3:15). The American landscape is not as religiously homogeneous as it was even a generation ago. In fact, we live in a culture that has critically and harshly scrutinized Christian claims for more than a century.

This environment of criticism and the dearth of biblical knowledge challenge Christians to leave behind our complacency about giving answers about our faith in God. Current popular atheist authors proclaim a bitter and mean dogmatism against people of faith. As Christian members of the same human community as these new atheists, we are responsible to stand up for the reasonableness of hope in God and to do so with the gentleness and respect due to our fellow man. This is to be done in such a way that "when you are slandered, those who revile your good behavior in Christ may be put to shame" (1 Peter 3:16). We are not to fear people, but we are to be constant reminders that there is a God, and He is Lord.

When I approach a particular women's ministry about teaching apologetics, I first establish the current cultural environment and remind women that they must actively participate in the forming of our culture rather than pulling away from it in complacency or fear. Women generally know and understand that this must be done, but a leader in the church will have to come alongside and remind them to take their place of influence as Christians in their communities. Apologetics studies will help alleviate their fears of interacting with others in an environment that can be hostile toward God.

With this groundwork laid, we need to help women understand how their beliefs affect every aspect of their lives (see chapters 1–3). Women affect everyone around them with their beliefs about God; this can be good or bad. So, when establishing an apologetics ministry, it is just as important to emphasize the role apologetics plays in the spiritual transformation of the believer as it is to emphasize having an answer for those who question our faith.

Women must understand that the things they habitually think about are the things that will guide her actions. This is vitally important to becoming a mature Christian. Consider how important the life of the mind was to Paul. He encourages the Philippians, "Finally, brothers, whatever is true, whatever is honorable, whatever is just, whatever is pure, whatever is lovely, whatever is commendable, if there is any excellence, if there is anything worthy of praise, think about these things" (Phil. 4:8). We are not told to accept whatever is mediocre or average in our society. We are told to go beyond these things toward those that are excellent and praiseworthy. In establishing the need for apologetics, we must constantly inspire our ladies to go beyond their current learning level toward higher and more excellent thoughts. Many churches advertise "Come just as you are" as a way to draw in people who might be uncomfortable in a church setting. I agree with this as an initial outreach, but once someone becomes a member, our motto should not be "Stay just as you are." If we fail to guide people forward to hard theology and difficult philosophies, we convey to them that they cannot handle it or we assume they are not interested in it.

To the leaders of women's ministries, I make an impassioned plea. Please understand that we create a shallow view of the Christian faith if we do not deal with difficult passages and tough questions. Look at the dilemma presented by the author of Hebrews who wants to teach in greater depth on the difficult concept of Jesus as the High Priest, but he cannot because the people have become dull of hearing. He rebukes, corrects, and criticizes them for not moving on to teaching positions themselves and for still needing the spiritual milk of young Christians (Heb. 5:11–14). If ladies in your church are using the idea of "a simple, child-like faith" as a reason not to learn hard Christian concepts, you need to help them see that childish thinking is not to be confused with the heart that trusts God with childlike faith (1 Cor. 3:2; Eph. 4:11–16). Be an encourager who rallies the troops toward learning the deep things of God. Find those in the women's ministry or in the church who have a desire to learn. Kindle in them a fire of interest in the teaching and learning of apologetics.

To the pastors in the church, I make my second plea. Have a specific and articulated goal for your women's ministry, one that includes apologetics as part of its educational plan. At the 2011 Southern Baptists of Texas Empower Evangelism Conference, Christian apologist Lee Strobel appealed to pastors in a keynote presentation. He said if he were a Texas pastor, he would do three things: (1) Put a new emphasis on apologetics; (2) Put a new emphasis on apologetics; and (3) Put a new emphasis on apologetics.

From experience, I understand that if a pastor encourages any movement in the church, it has much more of a chance to survive. Thus, I petition pastors to take an active role in the educational element of their flocks' ministries to women and to include the powerful teaching found in apologetics. We have an awesome opportunity laid before us in America. Resources abound—resources that can be used to train and transform women who will have an effective impact on their community. I am seeing a demonstrable difference in the women whose ministries have begun to study a defense of the faith; this difference results in a profound confidence in their belief in God.

There are a few ways to begin generating excitement for apologetics. One way is to bring in a guest speaker who can aptly communicate the need for apologetics. A local apologetics enthusiast would love to come discuss why this study is life changing. Most of my own speaking engagements in the last couple of years have been to introduce ministries, specifically women's ministries, to the field of Christian apologetics. Many people do not know much about apologetics at all, so we need to introduce it to them.

I cannot provide a foolproof guide to finding a local apologist that you can trust to be sound theologically and also able to relate to the women in your church, but I can offer some suggestions. First, check with your pastoral staff. Someone on staff or in the laity at your church may currently study apologetics and could be a good place to start. Second, if you belong to a denomination that has a local association, ask your associational staff for recommendations. Third, if you are near a seminary or Bible college, check their website for professors who teach philosophy, worldview, or apologetics courses. The school's Web site should include its doctrinal statement so you can check its theology, and it will usually also include professors' contact information. Fourth, you can check who is speaking at evangelical apologetics events. Some of these events include the Evangelical Philosophical Society's annual apologetics conference sponsored by Biola University and the National Conference on Christian Apologetics, sponsored by Southern Evangelical Seminary. There might also be local church conferences in your area.[1] The International Society of Women in Apologetics is a resource where you can find women who specifically speak in apologetics. If you utilize speakers with whom you are unfamiliar, either meet with them personally or talk to them on the phone. By doing so, you can get a feel for the individual speaker's personality and whether he or she would be a good fit for your women. An encouraging speaker will help generate an atmosphere of excitement through which you can introduce apologetics. If no one is available to come to you, get together a group from the church (don't forget to invite your pastor) and go to an apologetics conference in your area.

Ultimately, we aren't introducing apologetics to the church; we are reintroducing the church to apologetics, which is quite an old and effective endeavor in church history. The apostle Paul was known for making a defense, an *apologia*, of what he believed, such as before King Agrippa in Acts 26. The early church father, Justin Martyr, even wrote two treatises defending Christian beliefs entitled "First Apology" and "Second Apology" in the mid-second century.[2] We have the privilege of bringing back this great tradition in the church.

Another idea is to teach a discipleship course as an introduction. There are various apologetics organizations writing studies for just such a need.[3] Mikel Del Rosario has written an introductory work entitled *Accessible Apologetics*. His studies are some of the best introductory materials available and can be downloaded from his Web site (http://www.apologeticsguy.com). Another great beginning resource is the *Ambassador Basic Curriculum* from Stand to Reason Ministries (http://www.str.org). This is a compact disc course with online study

1. Evangelical Philosophical Society Conference: http://www.epsapologetics. com. the National Apologetics Conference: http://conference.ses.edu. Biola University conferences: http://www.biola.edu/academics/sas/apologetics/events. The International Society of Women in Apologetics: http:// womeninapologetics.com.

2. Justin Martyr's works can be read online at http://www.earlychristianwritings. com/justin.html.

3. These groups also take various approaches to apologetics, such as presuppositional, classical, evidentialist, and integrative. See "Suggested Resources" for specific studies.

tools and lecture notes. Plus, I have a curriculum geared towards women's bible studies entitled, *Why Do You Believe That?: A Faith Conversation* by LifeWay Press (2012). I have also seen ministries start book clubs that read apologetic works and then get together to discuss the chapters. Sometimes these clubs meet outside the church, such as at a bookstore or a coffee shop, and they take conversations on the arguments for and against God's existence out into the public square. Suggested books for reading can be found in the "Suggested Resources" list at the end of the book. Whatever you decide to do, one of the most important ways of generating excitement in the church is to have the pastor on board. When a pastor discusses the merits of an endeavor from the pulpit and is excited about an activity, the congregation will respond.

GOAL #2: CREATE THE ENVIRONMENT

In order to teach material that will help women grapple with their most difficult questions about belief in God, ministry leaders must provide them with a safe, loving, learning environment. Women need to know that the church is a place where they can ask questions, share doubts, and find answers. Additionally, they must be able to do so without fear of ridicule. Nearly every day in my seventh-grade algebra course, my teacher would ask us if there were any stupid questions. Then he would pause and say, "Mary Jo?" He pointed me out because I was known for asking any question, no matter how basic, that would help me better understand his teaching. Fortunately, I also remember other teachers who worked hard to guard an environment of learning and made sure their students had every opportunity to grow. Our church learning environments should be reminiscent of places like this, where discovery and learning were prized and protected aspects of the classroom. We should be careful to create optimal situations for women to investigate questions about God.

Although the perfect environment for learning will only be found on the other side of resurrection, there are several things you can do to help your church create a positive learning environment. The first of these may seem rudimentary, but it is critical: ask the church to pray. You can pray for the transformation of your local body of believers. Pray for the body to grow in spiritual maturity. According to Paul in Ephesians 4:11–13, Jesus has given the church the apostles, the prophets, the evangelists, the shepherds, and the teachers to equip the saints for the work of ministry. Their purpose in teaching is to help the church grow in the knowledge of the Son of God and mature into manhood.[4] So pray for a fire to be lit so that believers will begin to understand the necessity for spiritual maturity in their own lives and recognize that none of us has "arrived" or reached the pinnacle of our learning.

Next, pray for the unity of the believers in Christ. Earlier in the Ephesians 4 passage, Paul encourages the believers to be "eager to maintain the unity of the Spirit in the bond of peace" (Eph. 4:3). Commenting on this passage, Warren Wiersbe describes the meaning of Paul's words: "The verb used here is a present participle, which means we must constantly be endeavoring to maintain this unity. In fact, when we think the situation is the best, Satan will move in to wreck it. The spiritual unity of a home, a Sunday school class, or a church is the responsibility of each person involved, and the job never ends."[5] We have many things to pray for in the church, but the unity of the believers, specifically as they grow in spiritual maturity and knowledge, needs be a priority on our prayer lists. It is a characteristic of the church body that is so easily disrupted, yet so often forgotten in prayer.

Two final prayer preparations are to pray for the believers' minds to receive the truth and to pray for a willingness to learn. In John 17:17, Jesus prays, "Sanctify them in truth; your word is truth." So we should pray to be sanctified in truth, set apart from falsehood and worldliness, knowing and living out the gospel in truth and

---

4. I am avoiding the term *womanhood* here, which I think lends itself toward a misrepresentation of the text, even if just used for the appeal to women. Manhood refers to the maturity of the human being and is a trait to be sought by all.

5. Warren W. Wiersbe, *The Bible Exposition Commentary* (Wheaton, IL: Victor Books, 1996, 1989), ad loc. Eph 4:1.

righteousness (see also Ps. 25:4–5). I have tried not to focus too much on problems in the church throughout this book, but one area on which I will always comment when I teach is an unwillingness to learn. How can a woman actually call herself a follower of the most powerful Teacher the world has ever known if she has no commitment to learning? This does not make any sense. Consider this in a different context. For those of us who have children, which one of us would tell her child, "Hey, you don't need to continue to learn this stuff in school. You're good. As long as you think you've got the basics down, why continue to push yourself?" Yet how many of us in the church are modeling that very attitude toward learning about God? As Christians living in the twenty-first century, we have a world of knowledge at our fingertips. We have been given much and are responsible to use our resources wisely.[6] Take your place in the community as a believer in Christ; learn the theology!

The second idea for creating a learning environment involves identifying topics that might already be of interest to the women in your church. Make a survey listing apologetics issues, and then distribute the surveys to women in the church to complete and return for your leadership team's consideration. You could include topics such as the following:

- Does science make faith obsolete?

- Is there evidence for the resurrection?

- Are the Gospels historically reliable?

- How do I defend my faith to others?

- How can I have an open dialog with an atheist?

---

6. Jesus taught on this subject with the parable of the talents (Luke 19:11–27). Wiersbe observes in his commentary, "The important thing is not how much ability you have but how faithful you are to use what you have for the Lord" (*The Bible Exposition Commentary*, ad loc. Luke 19:11).

- Is life absurd without God?

- Can you give me a brief introduction to apologetics?

- What is "faith"?

- How can I learn to critically analyze arguments for and against the existence of God?

- How can God be good when there is evil in the world?

- Why affirm Christianity when there are so many other belief systems?

Such a survey not only discovers the interests of your women, but it helps create excitement about the subject being taught. Surveys can be handed out in Sunday school or Bible study groups, inserted in bulletins, e-mailed to church members, posted to a church Facebook group, or through the good old-fashioned, person-to-person survey in the hallway (how I did my first survey). Design the survey so individuals can rate the issues in order of interest. Then compile the results and assess your (or another person's) ability to teach in these areas. If at all possible, teach on the issues that interest your church the most in order to really build excitement about apologetics. Fashioning a course that speaks to women's existing interests guarantees that they will already be committed to the subject.

I suggest the survey method, as opposed to simply conducting a general apologetics study, unless your church indicates an interest in general apologetics (by checking the "Can you give me a brief introduction to apologetics" or "how do I defend my faith to others " options on the list). Be mindful that it can take a couple of weeks for the surveys to be fully completed, especially if you are using social media or e-mail. If you have distributed them through classes or bulletins, give a quick and upbeat reminder in the worship service about the surveys each week at church. Ask the women to take two minutes to fill out the survey and drop it off immediately following the service. If you have used social media or e-mail, send out reminders once a week, posting when the survey will be over and when classes will begin.

Finally, as you seek to create an environment for studying apologetics, remember to prepare your own heart and mind to lead. If you have been given the opportunity to be a leader in your church or community, please do not take this responsibility lightly. James 3:1 admonishes us, "Not many of you should become teachers, my brothers, for you know that we who teach will be judged with greater strictness." It is not enough for those who want to lead to expect that our knowledge or excitement will be enough. We must also aspire to lead through our own personal transformation; we must expect to grow along with those in the ministry. The teacher must be teachable, one who is open to constructive criticism. Leadership calls for accountability; if you put yourself above reproof, you are setting yourself up for failure. In addition, during the course of teaching apologetics, the teacher will encounter difficult issues as well as disagreements on certain issues. The teacher must be prepared to challenge others to support their views (as per "Action #3: Question" in chapter 4) and to mediate between views. Situations may arise in which you need to teach others how to handle disagreements, instead of teaching the material. Presenting an argument must not turn into arguing.

At a conference in Houston, I was speaking to women on the topic of "Truth and Tolerance" at a church leadership convention. After I had finished, a lady attending the session told me she greatly disagreed with my teaching and suggested that I was simply teaching people to argue. She requested that I stop my ministry because, she said, it is not biblical to argue. In my response, I first asked her to show me in the Scriptures where it was ungodly to argue, because it was important to me that she use Scripture to make such a strong rebuke. She said she would not do so and that I was to be quiet and listen to her. As the leader in the room that day, I realized quickly that my goal was to demonstrate a gracious but responsible way of handling such a disagreement since numerous women were still standing around. I wanted to demonstrate three principles in my response:

(1) we should correct people from the Scriptures; (2) we should hold people accountable for what they say; and (3) we can do both without creating a bad situation (Eph. 4:15). Afterward, thankfully, this is what the women who witnessed the encounter told me they perceived in my response. One woman even told me she was dealing with a similar situation and needed to know how I handled this overt rebuke.

By the end of the conversation, I established that I would not heed a rebuke that was (1) based solely in her personal opinion rather than in the Scriptures and (2) not interactive with the actual material I taught (it became apparent that she did not listen to my presentation). She asked me to consider giving up my teaching if two other people were ever to confirm her request because she believed in the confirmation of three. I told her many more people had affirmed my ministry, so that by her standard of the confirmation of three, I should continue with my teaching. She did not refute this statement; instead we had a few more polite exchanges on our differing views. We agreed to disagree and parted in relatively good humor. There were women who stayed all the way through our conversation, including the lady's friend. Her friend afterward thanked me for my presentation, and appeared grateful that I didn't take offense at the rebuke. If you are going to teach apologetics, know that disagreements are inevitable, and this is okay. How you handle the disagreement is often more important than the actual disagreement.

In an article titled "Advice to Christian Apologists," Christian philosopher and renowned apologist William Lane Craig advises:

> Be mindful of your personal, spiritual formation. In the end the most important thing is not what you do, but who you are. I'm not always enthusiastic when I meet a student who tells me that he wants to become a Christian apologist. One sometimes detects that what the student really wants is the limelight and the glory. Or there may be a spirit of argumentativeness or arrogance about him. Or perhaps a craving for the affirmation of others to offset a personal sense of inferiority. Of course, we

are all broken people, and none of us has motives
that are wholly pure. But it is vitally important that,
as a public representative of Christ, the Christian
apologist be a person who is filled with the Holy
Spirit and walking humbly with God.[7]

Though Dr. Craig is specifically addressing the individual apologist, his point has relevance to our subject of women's ministry. The task of implementing apologetics in women's ministry must be undertaken out of a true concern for the spiritual growth of the people God has entrusted to your leadership. The apostle Paul expresses this well in 2 Corinthians 2:4, "For I wrote to you out of much affliction and anguish of heart and with many tears, not to cause you pain but to let you know the abundant love that I have for you."

The reason we bring apologetics into our ministries is out of a passionate love for believers, not for selfish gain. Therefore, I advise leaders that their own lives must be constantly open to loving correction from our co-laborers in Christ, so that we as leaders will grow and learn, too. By taking your own spiritual development seriously, you will be better prepared to answer anyone in a way that is consistent with the character of a follower of Christ.

GOAL #3: FIND OR CREATE A STUDY

For most of the last decade, I have written my own materials for discipleship courses I have taught in the church. I did this because of the specific interests of my church and the lack of available resources. However, the situation has changed, and there is now a good selection of introductory apologetics materials available. These studies are not specifically aimed at women's ministry, but they are good beginning resources for any kind of group. I suggest a few great resources:

---

7. William Lane Craig, "Apologetics Training–Advice to Christian Apologists," Reasonable Faith, accessed March 27, 2011, http://www.reasonablefaith.org/site/News2?page=NewsArticle&id=5341.

- *Tactics: A Game Plan for Discussing Your Christian Convictions* by Gregory Koukl. Book and interactive DVD for small group study.

- *The Reason for God: Belief in an Age of Skepticism* by Timothy Keller. Book and DVD with study guide.

- *The Case for Christ: A Journalist's Personal Investigation of the Evidence for Jesus* by Lee Strobel. Book, DVD, and participants guide.

- *On Guard: Defending Your Faith with Reason and Precision* by William Lane Craig.

- *Know Why You Believe* by Paul E. Little. Book and study guide.

- *Why Do You Believe That? A Faith Conversation* by Mary Jo Sharp. Bible study, video-driven curriculum

These are introductory level and lay-friendly apologetics studies that will help get your women's ministry started in the defense of the Christian faith. The studies can be utilized with various sized groups within your women's ministry.

If you want to create a study on a particular topic that your survey identified, you can do so through your own study of Scriptures, articles online, and books.[8] Read through the material, taking notes on the important themes and issues. Study the Word to verify each concept. Create an outline from your notes for each session, and cover no more than three main points in some detail. Insert some questions near the end of each main point for the purpose of monitoring the group's understanding of that point. Then leave time for more general questions and answers at the end of each session.

---

8. See Suggested Resources at the end of this book for recommend
trusted Web sites to begin your study.

Before you teach these outlines, have a trusted friend look over the material for grammatical, theological, and philosophical editing. It would be wise to have your pastor review your outlines, so the leadership knows exactly what is being taught. These tailor-made studies can be very effective because they directly address issues in which your group has already expressed an interest. You can also create a study by finding a book on apologetics that addresses many of the topics from your survey. Authors Paul Copan and Kenneth Samples have excellent books for treating individual topics, one per chapter, with discussion questions at the end of each chapter.

These ideas are simply to help you start incorporating apologetics into your ministry. There is much more that you can do than what I have mentioned here. Although I would love to say, "Now go get started," we have one more area to think about: handling some objections that may come your way.

GOAL #4: ANSWER POSSIBLE OBJECTIONS

Most likely, since you are reading this book, you are already excited to bring the study of apologetics back into the church. However, your excitement for this endeavor will probably be met with a few objections. Some of these objections are due to misperceptions by people who have never encountered apologetics face-to-face. Some come from folks who have had bad experiences with apologists or in the area of apologetics. And some people have no background in apologetics whatsoever. We should be able, in these situations, to offer an apologetic for apologetics. We should have an answer for those who may bring up issues about teaching apologetics in church. Most of the following objections are ones I have specifically addressed over the past few years.

Objection #1: Apologists just want to win arguments.

This objection has a subtle nuance. "Winning" arguments in the sense of having a responsibly evidenced position that demonstrates itself to be the more coherent option for belief is a good goal. "Winning" arguments in the sense of having a feeling of domination over another person is not a good goal. The second position is more likely the nuance of this objection. Being belligerently and obnoxiously argumentative is not condoned in the Bible. However, it is worth noting that being an apologist does not entail that one must argue ungraciously. There are apologists who unfortunately are also argumentative. Conversely, there are apologists who are gracious and humble and who accept constructive criticism and correction with humility. This objection is a broad generalization based on an error in reasoning and ignoring of counterexamples. It paints all apologists with the same broad brush, when really there are many different personalities among apologists.

Furthermore, the New Testament authors, specifically Paul, actually commend interacting with arguments. In 2 Corinthians 10:4–5, he says, "For the weapons of our warfare are not of the flesh but have divine power to destroy strongholds. We destroy arguments and every lofty opinion raised against the knowledge of God, and take every thought captive to obey Christ."

This objection assumes the motive for a person's engagement with apologetics is to win arguments. However, some apologists became involved in their study because they wanted to answer their own doubts or the doubts of loved ones. They continue to do their work to provide good answers for themselves or for others. My own story is one of looking to answer the doubts that I had about God. Further, many apologists are just interested in sharing the good news of Jesus Christ and this is the way they have chosen to do so.

Objection #2: Apologists are trying to argue people into the kingdom of heaven.

This objection represents a mistaken perception concerning the work of apologetics. In making a defense of Christian beliefs, the apologist hopes to answer questions that may keep people from openly considering belief in God as a viable option for their lives. The apologist also aims to provide answers to doubts that Christians may have about the validity of their own beliefs in God, thus giving Christians more confidence in their faith.

Apologetics provides an *apologia*, a case or defense, for why a person believes in God. It can help in evangelism as it gives specific reasons for why a person believes God is real. However, the Christian apologist ultimately considers belief in God to be a response to the Holy Spirit drawing a person to God.

Objection #3: If you don't have anything nice to say, you shouldn't say anything at all.

It is deeply concerning to me that people say we shouldn't engage in the reasoning of our faith because it may lead to some disagreements in the church. The aim of this objection is what might be called "keeping the peace." Such reasoning says it is better to be nice and for everybody to get along than to discuss things that might upset some people.

The first problem with this sort of peace-keeping is that it is simply not biblical. The example of the apostle Paul was one of great love for the church, but he also had a great love for the truth. He was willing to speak truth even when it hurt the people in the church to hear it. In 2 Corinthians 1:23–2:1, Paul speaks of his relationship with the church at Corinth: ". . . it was to spare you that I refrained from coming again to Corinth. Not that we lord it over your faith, but we work with you for your joy, for you stand firm in your faith. For I made up my mind not to make another painful visit to you." Apparently, Paul's words to the Corinthians were harsh enough to cause him to write about not wanting to hurt them again with his presence. What we can take from Paul's example is that we must use *wisdom* in how we approach subjects that may have a history in the church or may be offensive to some folks. However, we should not let this objection stifle our entire endeavor to engage the subject of doubts and difficult questions about God. If Jesus is the embodiment of truth (John 14:6), we must be able to discuss and discover that truth. Otherwise, what we have is not really truth at all.

Objection #4: We should just give people the gospel.

"While I'm glad you are teaching the apologetics course, I don't need all that head knowledge. I just give people the gospel of Jesus." I have encountered this objection a few times from well-intentioned people who desire for the good news of Jesus Christ to be central in their message to others. However, I want to bring to mind a few considerations. First, the gospel of Jesus entails knowledge of certain propositions that another person may or may not believe. When we proclaim the gospel, we assume the historical reality of Jesus' life, humanity, and deity. We also assume the historical truth of Jesus' death and resurrection,[9] the existence of God, and the problem of a sinful human nature. Finally, we assume the reliability and authority of the Bible.

If people have never been exposed to some of these ideas, these principles may sound somewhat foreign or confusing to them. When our message seems hard for our listeners to understand, instead of walking away from the conversation and telling ourselves that they just were not ready to receive the gospel, we can help them with questions they may have on these issues. I'm not downplaying the role of the Holy Spirit, because I again affirm that the Holy Spirit is responsible to draw people to Himself. However, we miss out on a great opportunity to learn and grow with other people when we adopt a dismissive attitude toward people who may just have a few important questions about our beliefs.

Second, the gospel message itself is not magical and has no magical powers. Human verbalization of the gospel is not the same as the redemptive work of the Trinity. Our role is to share the gospel; only God can save. I meet many people each year who want so desperately to lead a person to the saving knowledge of God. This desire pleases our Father, but the knowledge of salvation that brings a person into right standing with God is His to give, not ours. Salvation is between a person and the Creator.

---

9. See the survey topics list on page 104

Objection #5: Arguing is against the teachings of the New Testament.

In Acts 19:8, we read that the apostle "Paul entered the synagogue and spoke boldly there for three months, arguing (διαλέγομαι; dialegomai) persuasively about the kingdom of God" (NIV). Apollos also "vigorously refuted his Jewish opponents in public debate, proving from the Scriptures that Jesus was the Messiah" (Acts 18:28, NIV). Paul and Apollos engaged in public arguing, following the example of their Lord Jesus Christ (Matt. 22–23).

However, we should actively avoid personal disputes and hostility as we address and analyze each others' beliefs. Arguing can be done in a way that is appropriate and godly when we do it in a spirit of humility, recognizing our own propensity for poor reasoning and error. If we admit where we are wrong in our thinking, we will be more approachable for those who want to discuss questions about God. Arguing, as it pertains to defending the principles of our faith, is not an unbiblical practice when governed by humility.

CLOSING ARGUMENT

Being argumentative does not fit into our women's ministries, but the arguing—the contending for the faith—that the first generation of believers engaged in was not childish one-upmanship rooted in a selfish desire to get one's own way. Just as an attorney argues a client's case before a judge and jury, we as Christians argue our case before a lost and dying world.

Long gone are the days when those we would witness to had, at the very least, a fundamental understanding of the God of the Bible and the message He gave us through Scripture. The influx of new immigrants from different religious backgrounds into our large cities provides a greater need for more American Christians to pursue biblical training. Though we may feel well equipped to share the gospel with a child during Vacation Bible School, can we adequately share that same message with our Hindu coworkers or our Muslim neighbors?

This is why it is so important to study the truth of our faith through apologetics. By studying and concisely conveying the historical, philosophical and logical context of Scripture we can help people understand who God is and why He can be trusted. And in doing so we give them the context in which to better understand the story of our God and His love for us as revealed in Scripture.

That is an argument worth winning.

PUTTING IT ALL TOGETHER

The practical implementation of apologetics in women's ministries must start in the lives of the leaders. The leaders' hearts must yearn to grow and learn as they stretch themselves out of their comfort zones. When our pastors work together with women's ministry leaders to create an atmosphere of excitement about learning, we achieve potentially infectious results. Perhaps your pastoral staff and ministry team could read an apologetics book together before beginning the push for apologetics among your ladies. What an amazing impact such a show of solidarity would have on a women's ministry. Invite the pastor to drop in during your women's study classes and give a plug for apologetics. Can you imagine how greatly women would be encouraged to take part in a study that even her pastor found inspiring? I can! I pray that this situation will become more frequent in our churches.

If you plan to introduce apologetics with the help of your women's ministry team or with just another woman or two who are excited about apologetics, go through the material as a small study group before teaching it to the entire ministry. Together you can discuss the ideas and solidify important points before you try to teach the larger group. As you bounce your ideas off a couple others, invite your pastor to share constructive criticism as well. The more people you can find who are likeminded, the more enthusiasm you will generate for this new endeavor. Don't forget that your family can also be a great source of support to help you engage the topics and rally excitement. I often discuss current topics with both my husband and daughter. After you have laid all your groundwork through praying, garnering support, getting people excited, creating a safe learning environment, and finding a study, you have one last preparation: thank the Lord that He has given His people such an incredible opportunity to learn!

Chapter 6

THE TESTIMONY OF WOMEN

*For the women of those days were more
spirited than lions, sharing with the Apostles
their labors for the Gospel's sake.*
—John Chrysostom, Archbishop of Constantinople,
4th century

The things we have been considering are not revolutionary ideas for the body of Christ; they are reminders of ancient teachings that we already know. And just as I encourage others to follow these principles, I must continually remind myself as well! Like everyone else, I wrestle with the tendency to be proud, to make generalizations, to be judgmental, and to be distracted by worldly desires that lead me away from good reasoning and a loving spirit. So in no way do I want to downplay how much sin influences our lives. It would be a mistake to think if someone simply follows the suggestions in this book that—all of a sudden—life will be nothing but happiness and bliss. My primary goal has been to move us toward honesty with ourselves in order that the truth of Christ's teaching might transform our lives first and then spread outward to affect our families, neighborhoods, communities, and beyond.

Throughout this book, I have emphasized the importance of a woman's ability to defend what she believes. We've looked at

(1) questioning why a person believes in God (chapter 1); (2) the implications of true belief in God (chapters 2 and 3); (3) how to begin talking about beliefs in everyday conversations (chapter 4); and (4) how to implement the study of apologetics in women's ministries (chapter 5). We'll conclude with one final reason for this book: helping women taking their place in the kingdom as influential citizens of their communities and giving testimony to the risen Jesus.

An important part of being influential in our communities involves breaking down negative stereotypes of Christianity. The negative view of evangelicals in the American academic setting necessitates a thoughtful response from all of us. In his book *Christians Are Hate-Filled Hypocrites . . . and Other Lies You've Been Told*, Bradley R. E. Wright cites statistics from an Institute for Jewish and Community Research study on the view of religious groups. When 12,000 college professors were asked if they had negative feelings toward certain religious groups, 53 percent of the respondents affirmed having negative feelings toward evangelical Christians, the highest ranking on the survey. The next closest was the Mormons with just over 30 percent, and Jews were last with only 3 percent.[1] Contrarily, when the general public was asked the same question, only 32 percent reported an unfavorable view of evangelical Christians.[2] The highest concentration of unfavorable views of evangelicals lies in the academic arena.

There are two correlations to women's ministry indicated by Wright's conclusions. First, as parents, mentors, teachers, and friends of young people in the church, women must realize that we are sending our Christian students into this unreceptive academic arena. Are we preparing them with good reasoning that is not just based in curriculum or teaching but is also based in our own individual

---

1. Bradley R. E. Wright, *Christians Are Hate-Filled Hypocrites . . . and Other Lies You've Been Told: A Sociologist Shatters Myths from the Secular and Christian Media* (Minneapolis, MN: Bethany House, 2010), 205–6.

2. Ibid., 197–98. Of the 32 percent of non-Christian respondents with an unfavorable view of evangelicals, the majority (45 percent) were over the age of 50. If Wright's findings are indicative of reality, then perhaps we should emphasize reaching the "last generation" as well as the "next generation."

use of good reasoning? Are we modeling good thinking? As an educator, I've often observed how much more students learn and retain when their teachers genuinely love and live out what they teach. If the church does not demonstrably show critical reasoning ability and a love of learning—or if rational analysis is partitioned off from life in Christ—students will not consider good reasoning to be an essential part of their Christian walk. This refers not only to teenage students, but to adults as well. Adults need to understand that good reasoning and the Christian faith go hand-in-hand. Although not all women in the church are university students or academic professionals, all women in the church are students of life and disciples of Christ.

Second, as a nation we've revered our universities as American pillars of freedom of speech, tolerance, and the exploration of ideas. They are iconic to our culture whether or not we have gone to college. Their ideology affects all of us, either directly through attendance or indirectly through their influence on culture. Yet the university is proving to be one of the most negative environments toward evangelical Christianity. How should the evangelical community respond to those who view them so negatively? As women, we are a part of that community, and we are responsible to respond. By training women to question others (see chapter 4) and by facilitating their role as studied, thoughtful believers in God, women's ministries can significantly combat our culture's misperceptions. Conversely, if a woman's ministry disconnects Christian women from unbelievers in an "us versus them" mentality, mocks or belittles academic endeavor, or treats fellowship as a place to hide from the criticisms of outsiders, then it is not the kind of ministry that will equip Christians to influence their culture or minister to their communities. We should bravely and graciously transgress these man-made boundaries with the understanding that all people are working through life together. It is not Christians versus non-Christians.[3] It's time to take some risks in women's ministry.

---

3. Bradley's statistics also show that evangelical Christians have more of a negative view of atheists than vice versa.

SPIRITED AS LIONS

When early church father John Chrysostom wrote, "For the women of those days were more spirited than lions, sharing with the Apostles their labors for the Gospel's sake," he was commenting on the apostle Paul's high praise for Priscilla (Prisca) in Romans 16:3–4. Paul says, "Greet Prisca and Aquila, my fellow workers in Christ Jesus, who risked their necks for my life, to whom not only I give thanks but all the churches of the Gentiles give thanks as well." Out of her love for Jesus, Priscilla was willing to lay her life down for her friend, Paul. Jesus says there is no greater love (John 15:13). What a great example for women today! Priscilla lived in a time when the Jews and Christians were ordered out of Rome. They experienced persecution under the Roman Emperor Claudius. She responded to her cultural circumstances by offering her life for the safety of Paul's because of her belief in God. In comparison, how very little God asks of us today when He asks us to be risk-takers in early twenty-first-century America by standing up to false ideas about our faith.

In his homily on the book of Acts, Chyrsostom comments on this passage:

> For what is greater or so great, as to have been a succorer[4] of Paul? at her own peril to have saved the teacher of the world? And consider: how many empresses there are that no one speaks of. But the wife of the tent-maker is every where reported of with the tent-maker (meaning perhaps St. Paul); and the width that the sun sees over, is no more of the world than what the glory of this woman runneth unto. Persians, and Scythians, and Thracians, and they who dwell in the uttermost parts of the earth, sing of the Christian spirit of this woman, and bless it. How much wealth, how many diadems and purples

---

4. A succorer is one who helps or aides.

would you not be glad to venture upon obtaining
such a testimony?"[5]

The memories of these great empresses have dimmed, yet Priscilla's
fame lives and shines as a testimony of her faithful service to the King
of everlasting glory. In comparison to the risk-taking and influence of
the earliest Christian women, we have our job cut out for us.

I recently had lunch with my friend Amanda, who mentioned
she had spoken with a couple of women in the church about going
out to the mission field. When they came to the subject of having
children, one of the ladies said, "Oh, but then you'll have to wait to
have children. It's too dangerous for them on the mission field." This
attitude perplexed Amanda. "Mary Jo," she asked, "since when did
being a Christian become associated with avoiding peril in this life?
Christianity is not safe."

Ladies, the one charge that I can give you is to stop viewing your
faith, your church, and your women's ministry as providing you with
a neat, tidy package of safety and security in this life. This is not the
abundant and adventurous life to which we have been called. When
we become comfortable in our women's ministries, we become ineffective. The Lord never said that taking up our cross daily would be
comfortable, but He did promise to send the Comforter, the Holy
Spirit, to renew, uplift, and lead us into wisdom and give us the power
to obey the commands of Jesus. Those commands include (1) loving
God with all your heart, soul, and mind (Matt. 22:37); (2) loving
your neighbor as you love yourself (Matt. 22:39); (3) loving other
Christians (John 17:21–24); and (4) making disciples of all nations
(Matt. 28:19–20). In order to do these things we are going to have to
engage our ministries in some "risky business."

What's so risky about the business of going about the Lord's commands? If we consider these commands carefully, we will see more
clearly. To love God with all our heart, soul, and mind, means that
we give over all we have and all we are to the Lord. To faithfully
follow this command, we cannot overlook any nook or cranny in

---

5. Philip Schaff, *The Nicene and Post-Nicene Fathers*, 551.

our lives. We *will* be uncomfortable when we stop excusing our sins and honestly present each aspect of our fallen nature to the Lord for transformational redemption. We are putting ourselves in peril each day when we take up the challenge of Jesus' cross of sacrifice because it means death to the selfishness and the worldly mindset that hinders wholehearted devotion to God.

To love our neighbors as ourselves demands further risk. We don't need a scientist to tell us that no two humans are exactly alike. Just put two people in a room together for an hour and their differences will rapidly surface. The risk in loving our neighbor is that we might get hurt or we might hurt someone. Nevertheless, if we don't take this risk of facing conflict, how can we be peacemakers who reflect the character of Christ, the Mediator who brings peace between God and humankind?

Demonstrably loving other Christians involves an enormous threat to our pride. An atheist shared an old joke with me once, saying "Christians are like a group of porcupines in the North Pole. They all huddle together for warmth, but then they prick each other to death." What a grievous indictment! How thoroughly necessary it is for us to humbly love one another, to bless and to encourage, to teach and to exhort, to patiently discipline and eagerly seek to restore those in error, and to compassionately serve the poor and the needy in our ranks that the world might see the testimony of God's risen Son in our relationships with one another.

We need to take an honest look at women's ministries and ask how—or if—they are effectively making disciples of all nations. The ministry of women in the New Testament keenly focuses on mission work in the surrounding community as well as around the world. Currently, we see a great emphasis on encouraging one another through fellowship, which is important but is not the end in itself. We strengthen each other within our fellowship so that we can move beyond our comfort zones and be blessings in our communities. I suggest a revival of the evangelistic emphasis within women's ministries, a revival that includes both apologetics as discipleship and includes mission work that permeates our immediate surroundings, in addition to overseas. Get back to the basics of the hard doctrinal truths. Get women to analyze their lives to know whether they actually believe what they claim. Train them how to stand their intellectual ground and even advance against worldly pretensions. Take them out into the community to do good works and to spread the good news. Take some new risks by bringing together your women's ministry and your community. And most certainly, give women uncomfortable, "risky" opportunities to testify to the most important event in human history: the resurrection of the Lord Jesus Christ.

As a part of this goal, I again encourage women in the church to engage in the cultural battle for truth. Wherever did the idea come from that women should just be saccharine Christians who play out their beliefs over in the corner away from all the normal kinds of people unless they are doing a specific evangelistic push at the church?[6] This is downright weird, ladies. You are a part of the human race with complexity of thoughts, feelings, and beliefs, just like anyone else out there. You were created to be a valuable contributor to your community and to the whole of humankind. Your ideas should be discussed and constructively criticized just like the ideas of anyone else. Your inherent value demands that you discover why you hold your beliefs to be true.

GOD VALUES THE TESTIMONY OF WOMEN

In February of 2010, I debated a Muslim woman on the subject "The View of Women in the Qur'an and Bible." The debate was sponsored by the North American Muslim Foundation and was held in a mosque in Toronto, Ontario. On the night of the debate, we packed the main prayer room. So many people showed up that the mosque ran out of chairs! As I set up my materials and surveyed the attendees, I realized that at least 85 percent of the audience was Muslim. I asked God for calmness and assurance about the rigorous debate in which I was about to engage.

I had been nervous the entire week leading up to the debate.

---

6. I know there are means of tracing the course of Christian influence in the American (colonial) culture over the last 200–300 years. My statement is more rhetorical in nature for the purpose of challenging a current trend.

I could barely eat or sleep, constantly worrying about my material and my responses to my opponent's material. Entrenched in piles of papers and books at night, I wrestled with what I could present as the main difference between the views. I had been through the creation account, the activities of women in the Old and New Testaments, the description of the woman in Proverbs 31, the responsibility of a husband to love a wife as he loves his own body in Ephesians 5, and much more.

All of these topics made for great argumentation, but the one thing that stood above all others was the testimony of the women about the risen Jesus. This was going to be an important point to drive home with my Muslim audience. Muhammad said a woman's testimony is only worth half of a man's testimony because she lacks common sense.[7] According to the Qur'an (Surah 2:282), due to her forgetfulness a woman cannot even be trusted to testify alone about a fixed debt contract, so two women must testify if there is not a man available. Muhammad further explained that a woman's lack of common sense was so bad that it was part of the reason for why women constitute a majority of those in hell![8]

What a contrast between this view and that of the Lord Jesus Christ. Women were the first to find the empty tomb and to testify to the foundational doctrine of the Christian faith: the physical resurrection of Jesus Christ. In Christianity, a woman's testimony and intellect were trustworthy enough to bear witness to the greatest event in human history. God broke cultural norms by giving these first-century women a responsibility to testify about His most awesome work of redemption.

It is remarkable to find women in the Passion narratives as primary witnesses, testifying to the resurrection of Jesus (Matt. 28:1–10). It is so unusual, in fact, that it fulfills one criterion for establishing an event as historical: the principle of embarrassment. Because of the low status of a woman's testimony in first-century Jewish culture, the testimony of the women would not help build the first Christians' case

---

7. *Sahih Muslim* 142, book 1, number 142 (Siddiqui translation).
8. Ibid.

for the truthfulness of the empty tomb or the risen Jesus. Rather, their testimony in that culture should have harmed the disciples' witness. As the Jewish historian Josephus wrote, "But let not the testimony of women be admitted, on account of the levity and boldness of their sex, nor let servants be admitted to give testimony on account of the ignobility of their soul; since it is probable that they may not speak truth, either out of hope of gain, or fear of punishment."[9] Finding women in this honored role is so countercultural to the society that initially received the story from the disciples that its embarrassing quality cues historians that it is true. The revelation the women at the tomb received was the foundational doctrine of the Christian faith. God trusted and greatly used the testimony of these women.

My intent is not to use this event in the gospel story as an argument for or against the differing views of the roles of women in the church, or as a response to attacks against the church concerning the view of women. To do so, might make more of this aspect of the Gospel narratives than was intended by the authors. Rather, it is a fact of the gospel story that women were the first recipients of and testifiers to the knowledge that Jesus had risen from the dead. My use of this example is meant to reaffirm the woman's significance as *a Christian* in spreading the testimony of the risen Lord and Savior. God does not view her testimony as a woman's testimony is viewed in Islam, as untrustworthy or insufficient. I hope you can hear my heart in this matter, which is to encourage women in the bold proclamation of truth in the public square.

Let's consider examples of other women in the New Testament. Returning to the example of Priscilla in the book of Acts, we find her and her husband helping correct the teaching of the powerful preacher and great man of the Scriptures, Apollos. Priscilla was apparently well disciplined and learned enough to aid in this correction; this is particularly impressive given the cultural view of women in her time. In the story of the woman and Jesus at the well in Samaria (John 4:4–42), the Samaritan woman runs back into town to testify

---

9. Flavius Josephus and William Whiston, *The Works of Josephus: Complete and Unabridged* (Peabody: Hendrickson, 1996), Ant. 4.219.

about Jesus saying, "Come, see a man who told me all that I ever did. Can this be the Christ?" The townspeople responded to her testimony by coming out to see Jesus. Another colleague of Paul, Phoebe was a member of the church in Cenchreae and was responsible for delivering the letter Paul wrote to the Romans (Rom. 16:1). Of this fact Warren Wiersbe exclaims, "Never did a messenger carry a more important letter!"[10] Anna, a prophetess in Jesus' day, had been a widow for eighty-four years. She lived in the temple, where she prayed and fasted every day. After Simeon's blessing on Jesus, Anna praised God for the baby and spoke of Him to all those who were gathered there (Luke 2:36–38). These women delivered the good news of God in powerful, influential, and even precarious ways. Above all these examples stand the women at the tomb and their excitement to run back and tell the disciples the pivotal news in the history of humankind that Jesus had risen from the dead.

There are many women's testimonies throughout history that we could discuss, but let's consider some examples from today. In what dynamic ways are women proclaiming the resurrection of the Lord Jesus? Just like Priscilla risked her life for the proclamation of the risen Lord, some women currently risk everything simply to profess their own belief in Jesus. Maryam Rustampoor, 29, and Marzieh Amirizadeh, 32, of Iran were sentenced to imprisonment for life because of their apostasy from Islam to the Christian faith. They were charged with being anti-government activists and spent 259 days in prison in Tehran in 2009.[11] Aasia Bibi, a 45-year-old Pakistani Christian mother of five, was sentenced to death in June 2009 for blasphemy after being accused by fellow field laborers of making derogatory remarks about Muhammad.[12] The reported incident

---

10. Wiersbe, *The Bible Exposition Commentary*, ad loc. Rom. 16:1.

11. Maryam Rustampoor and Marzieh Amirizadeh, interview by Sam Yeghnazar, "Iran: Life in Prison," Voice of the Martyrs, last modified July 12, 2011 http://www.persecution.com/public/newsroom.aspx?story_ID=NDAw.

12. "Christian Woman Sentenced to Death Under 'Blasphemy Law,'" Barnabas Aid, last modified December 1, 2010, https://barnabasfund.org/?m=7_percent2312&a=2018.

began when Aasia fetched water for her coworkers who then refused to drink it because Aasia was a Christian. The Federal Minister for Minority Affairs in Pakistan (also a Christian) denied that there was any blasphemy and cited the incident as a personal conflict, yet Aasia still awaits her sentence in prison. There has been an international outcry against the Pakistani government to reform the blasphemy law in light of Aasia's death sentence.

Other women here in the United States boldly stand for the truth of Jesus Christ by taking a stand in the marketplace of ideas. Janet Parshall and Nancy Pearcey have both entered into public debate as evangelical Christian women discussing politics, art, media, philosophy, and theology in powerful ways. Pearcey has authored *Saving Leonardo: A Call to Resist the Secular Assault on Minds, Morals, and Meanings* and *Total Truth: Liberating Christianity from Its Cultural Captivity.* She has spoken to university students, actors and screenwriters, staffers at the White House and on Capitol Hill, as well as at many apologetics and worldview conferences. Pearcey has made appearances on National Public Radio and C-SPAN. *The Economist* has touted her as "America's pre-eminent evangelical Protestant female intellectual."[13] Janet Parshall takes to the airwaves on radio and television, going head-on into some highly intimidating circumstances on programs in which the host's ideology vehemently disagrees with her own (*Politically Incorrect, Larry King Live,* as well as other programs on CNN, MSNBC, CBS, ABC, NBC, and PBS). Her syndicated radio talk show, "In the Market with Janet Parshall," is broadcast on over six hundred stations. She has been honored by her peers for her prowess as a radio talk show host and for being "scrupulously fair" and intelligent.[14] Both of these women are examples of those who have taken their beliefs into the public square for testing. Both of

13. Nancy Pearcey, "Rallying to restore God," *The Economist*, last modified December 10, 2010, http://www.economist.com/blogs/prospero/2010/12/nancy_pearcey.

14. Adapted from Helen Kooiman Hosier, *100 Christian Women Who Changed the 20th Century* (Grand Rapids: Revell, 2000), 138–41.

these women boldly testify to the historical truth of the resurrection of Jesus.

So, what about us? God values and trusts the testimony of women, but what is your view of your own testimony? Do you think you have a valuable message to convey to people around you? Do you believe your words and actions matter? If God is real, then His message of the resurrection of Jesus in your testimony is of utmost importance.[15] It not only has real power to change lives, but it is also the most significant subject you can possibly discuss with anyone, anywhere, at any time. There is not some sort of textbook scenario in which our conversations will always be directly on the topic of God, or in which we employ a seven-step formula that results in the spiritual conversion of an unbeliever within five minutes. Realistically, since God is the Creator, we have access to many topics of discussion that can reveal His Spirit and truth: ethics, politics, economy, education, relationships, art, history, and nature. If we are honestly who we say we are—Christians—and we honestly and responsibly believe in God with all our mind, then we will not fear but rather welcome the kinds of conversations that lend themselves to intellectual debates over origins, meaning, and the afterlife.

THE NEED FOR WOMEN IN APOLOGETICS

We live in a culture in which women have a greater opportunity to voice their opinions and ideas than ever before. How are we using this gift that God has given us to benefit humankind? All Christians have been given the command by Jesus to make disciples of all nations (Matt. 28:19–20). It is not just a missionary's gift to evangelize and disciple; it is the work of the entire body of Christ.[16] So women, whether missionaries or not, also bear the responsibility to share and discover truth with others. Women (in the West) in modern times

---

15. When I use the word "testimony," I am including the evidence you have for the existence of God as well as your personal experience with Him.

16. I would argue that every member of the body of Christ is a "missionary." Here, I'm using a more traditional sense of the term.

have the most freedom and power of influence as we have seen in the history of humankind. This freedom comes with the responsibility to use it wisely. Implementing apologetics in women's ministries engages even more of the body of Christ in the action of actively spreading the Word of Truth. God has developed an army of truth-bearers in the church through women's ministries that regularly meet for encouragement and discipleship. Let us move the ministry out of boot camp and into the battle for truth.

In Ephesians 6, Paul uses an analogy of the Roman soldier's battle gear. Many Christians are familiar with this passage in which we find the "armor of God." We've no doubt heard many a sermon on how to "put on" this armor, but there's an interesting point in the passage that we may have missed. New Testament scholar Craig Keener writes specifically about three of the pieces of battle gear: the helmet of salvation, the breastplate of righteousness, and the sword of truth.

The Ephesians receiving this letter would have known that a Roman soldier only put on his helmet and breastplate for going into actual battle.[17] Paul uses these battle pieces in his analogy as the "putting on" of salvation and righteousness. The implication is that if you have the salvation of Jesus, you are placing yourself in battle. Since this was written to Ephesians who would have known that these pieces were for war, the purpose of the comparison for them would be that we are in warfare once we have the salvation and righteousness of Christ.

Keener then discusses the short Roman sword. The sword was only about twenty-four inches in length, and its primary purpose was for close engagement with the Roman enemy. Keener observes, "Thus Paul implies that the battle is to be joined especially by engaging those who do not know God's word (the gospel) with its message, after one is spiritually prepared in the other ways listed here. Paul's ministry was thus particularly strategic, because it included close-range battle advancing into enemy ranks (vv. 19–20)."[18] Notice, that Paul's analogy

---

17. Craig Keener, *The IVP Bible Background Commentary: New Testament* (Downers Grove, IL: InterVarsity Press, 1993), 554.

18. Ibid.

of the armor of God was not just intended to convey that Christians should protect themselves with righteousness and truth and faith, nor was it just for the building up of believers (discipleship). Rather, it was a reality check for the Ephesians that they have engaged in warfare for the truth by putting on the battle gear of Christ. "Therefore take up the whole armor of God, that you may be able to withstand in the evil day, and having done all, to stand firm" (Eph. 6:13).

Christian woman, you are a follower of Christ, and therefore you are engaged on the battlefield of ideology whether or not you realize it. What are you doing to prepare yourself for the fiery darts that come your way? Christ's call is to fight untruth, and engaging in battle is an act of love and mercy to those who oppose your beliefs. As Paul said, "For we do not wrestle against flesh and blood," but against the "spiritual forces of evil" (Eph. 6:12). This is why Jesus told us to love our enemies (Luke 6:27). We are not battling against people, but against untruth. Loving people involves sharing what is true in a strategic and winsome way.

Christian women are much needed and valuable members of the battle for truth. So if the church desires Christian women to contribute to the marketplace of ideas and be influential in their communities, then it must encourage a woman's biblical engagement in the discussion of truth. Indeed, the church should not just encourage this, but it should expect it from women as responsible and capable members of the Christian community. As a Christian family, we need to be gracious toward each other as we grow and learn together, not hastily leaping to severe conclusions about our fellow brothers and sisters in Christ. Rather, following the example of Priscilla and Aquilla with Apollos, Paul with the early churches, and Jesus with those whom He taught, we should help each other discover truth while purposefully demonstrating our love toward one another.

We have an opportunity before us to see effective and extensive changes in the lives of women in the church. I have already seen some of this happening in Texas, and the change has come along with hearts that desire to go deeper into theology, to learn about the foundations of beliefs, and to share their testimony with their communities. It is indeed exciting to be in the church while

Christian apologetics is making a return. As we study the defense of the faith and begin to engage our culture, we will see notable differences in ourselves and in our interaction with the community. We have a chance to take our place in society and reclaim a position of influence based in solid reasoning and confident faith. Perhaps, this is also a chance to remember who we are: active molders and shapers of the history of the world. Though the task of making a defense of the faith may seem great, the results have the potential for equal, if not more, greatness.

IN CONCLUSION

We've considered how the reasoning of beliefs can transform an individual and how answering why we believe is a part of being honest with ourselves and others. I heard this need for honesty expressed very succinctly by a panel of young women in their twenties at a state women's forum. When asked what the church could do better to relate to the younger generations, one young lady said, "We want Christians in the church to be real. We want to see that they really believe what they profess." She further expressed that one way of "getting real" was to provide answers to difficult questions about the faith. Then she smiled and said, "That's why it's important that we study apologetics." Knowing that I was at the conference, she added, "That was for you, Mary Jo Sharp!"

Studying apologetics can help women's ministries see foundational transformation in people's lives. Over and over, I have heard women say, "I'm not sure I know why I believe in God," and most of these women have not been young Christians. They were women who would say they have been Christians for decades. Yet, if a professing Christian doesn't know why she believes or what she believes, how can she say she really believes it? This was the overriding theme of the panel of twenty-somethings at the forum. They want to know how you know Jesus is the truth. They want to journey with you in finding the answers. And they want to see that knowledge manifest in the way you live, not as perfected beings, but as those who, in humility, desire to mature in their knowledge of God. They want to see you defend your knowledge and live it boldly *in public*. This is the key phrase for our women's ministries: going public with the faith.

Ultimately, however, my reasoning for apologetics study is not just because I am concerned for the younger generation or because I want to see Christian women become good thinkers who are emboldened with truth. It is because I desire to give God whatever glory I am able to with this life of mine. God gave me (and you) the gift of a rational mind; I will use that mind for Him. I don't always use good thinking and my family knows that I often reason badly. What I can do, though, is never stop learning, since I follow the greatest Teacher the world has ever known. My goal is to see real change, and I will journey toward that goal by changing myself first. I remain a healthy skeptic, but I will rush into the spiritual battle for truth with my heart, soul, and mind.

Suggested Resources

WHERE TO BEGIN

Learning Basic Christian Beliefs

These works will teach you the essential Christian doctrines, including the attributes of God.

"The Discipleship Program." *Reclaiming the Mind Ministries.*
   Available from http://www.reclaimingthemind.org. This DVD
   program with workbook covers the basic Christian beliefs.
Erickson, Millard J. *Christian Theology*. Grand Rapids: Baker, 1998.
   This book is a comprehensive treatment of the basic Christian
   beliefs.
_____. *An Introduction to Christian Theology*. Grand Rapids:
   Baker, 2001. This text is an abridged treatment of the basic
   Christian beliefs.
Grudem, Wayne. *Systematic Theology: An Introduction to Biblical
   Doctrine*. Grand Rapids: Zondervan, 1994. Grudem's book is
   an encyclopedic work on the basic Christian doctrines; easily searchable for answers to questions on the nature of God,
   nature of man, nature of Christ, and more.
Tozer, A. W. *The Knowledge of the Holy*. New York: Harper Collins,
   1961. This small book on the character of God has short chapters that each discuss one of God's attributes.

Learning a Defense of the Christian Faith

Here are some books to get started with reading in apologetics. The list is broken into three divisions: beginning, intermediate, and advanced.

Beginning

Bluedorn, Nathaniel, and Hans Bluedorn. *The Fallacy Detective: Thirty-Eight Lessons on How to Recognize Bad Reasoning.* Portland, OR: Christian Logic, 2009. This introduction to critical thinking is written for preteens through adults; use it to train your children as well as yourself.

Craig, William Lane. *On Guard: Defending Your Faith with Reason and Precision.* Colorado Springs, CO: David C. Cook, 2010. This accessible study offers arguments for God from one of the greatest Christian philosophers of our time.

Geisler, Norman L., and Frank Turek. *I Don't Have Enough Faith to Be an Atheist.* Wheaton, IL: Crossway, 2004. Geisler and Turek cover a broad spectrum of arguments in an introductory manner. I purchased this book for my mom!

Habermas, Gary R., and Michael R. Licona. *The Case for the Resurrection of Jesus.* Grand Rapids: Kregel, 2004. This book gives groundwork for belief in the historical reality of Jesus' resurrection.

Keller, Timothy. *The Reason for God: Belief in an Age of Skepticism.* New York: Riverhead, 2009. I suggest this book as a first read for beginners; it's apologetics from a pastor's perspective.

Koukl, Gregory. *Tactics: A Game Plan for Discussing Your Christian Convictions.* Grand Rapids: Zondervan, 2009. Koukl provides an easy and natural way to begin talking with others about your beliefs.

Newman, Randy. *Questioning Evangelism: Engaging People's Hearts the Way Jesus Did.* Grand Rapids: Kregel, 2004. Conversational skills are invaluable and necessary for good interaction with others. Newman is one of the best in this area.

Powell, Doug. *Holman QuickSource Guide to Christian Apologetics.* Nashville: Broadman & Holman, 2006. This is a basic overview of many apologetic subjects such as other religions, the problem of evil, the resurrection, and much more.

Strobel, Lee. *The Case for Christ: A Journalist's Personal Investigation of the Evidence for Jesus.* Grand Rapids: Zondervan, 1998. This is the first book I read all the way through in my attempt to answer my doubts. Highly suggested for beginners.

Zacharias, Ravi. *The End of Reason: A Response to the New Atheists.* Grand Rapids: Zondervan, 2008. Zacharias offers a response to Sam Harris's *Letter to a Christian Nation*, in which he exposes the poor reasoning in Harris's critique of Christianity.

Intermediate

Beckwith, Francis J., and Gregory Koukl. *Relativism: Feet Firmly Planted in Mid-Air.* Grand Rapids: Baker Books, 1998. This book is an in-depth refutation of the idea that "whatever truth works for you is good for you; whatever truth works for me is good for me."

Copan, Paul. *True for You, But Not for Me: Deflating the Slogans That Leave Christians Speechless.* Grand Rapids: Bethany House, 1998. This is one in a series of Copan books that take one objection or question per chapter and provides succinct answers.

_____. and William Lane Craig, eds. *Come Let Us Reason: New Essays in Christian Apologetics.* Nashville: B&H Academic, 2012. I have a chapter in this book so, naturally, it has to make the list! It's a great collection of essays on topics such as Did God Command Genocide of the Canaanites, Does the Old Testament Endorse Slavery, Does Jesus' Story Mimic Pagan Mystery Stories, the Silence of God, and many more.

Dembski, William A., and Michael R. Licona, eds. *Evidence for God: 50 Arguments for Faith from the Bible, History, Philosophy, and Science.* Grand Rapids: Baker, 2010. This is a collection of essays by top scholars arguing for the existence of God.

Evans, Craig A. *Fabricating Jesus: How Modern Scholars Distort the Gospels.* Downers Grove, IL: InterVarsity Press, 2008. This is a defense of the reliability of the Gospels and a refutation of the Gnostic Gospels.

Komoszewski, J. Ed, M. James Sawyer, and Daniel B. Wallace. *Reinventing Jesus: How Contemporary Skeptics Miss the Real Jesus and Mislead Popular Culture.* Grand Rapids: Kregel, 2006. The authors establish the reliability of the biblical texts.

Lewis, C. S. *Mere Christianity.* San Francisco: HarperCollins, 2001. Lewis's book is a foundational work in Christian apologetics that should be read by all Christians; arguments include the existence of a moral law, faith and reason, existence of virtue, and more.

Sire, James W. *The Universe Next Door: A Basic Worldview Catalog,* 4th ed. Downers Grove, IL: InterVarsity Press, 2004. Sire walks through how each worldview handles the toughest and most important questions about life; a foundational work for all Christians.

Zacharias, Ravi. *Can Man Live Without God.* Nashville: Thomas Nelson, 2004. This is an argument for the existence of God based on the absurdity of life without God; beautifully written.

Advanced

Bowman, Robert M., Jr., and J. Ed Komoszewski. *Putting Jesus in His Place: The Case for the Deity of Christ.* Grand Rapids: Kregel, 2007. This in-depth study explains how we know Jesus is God.

Craig, William Lane. *Reasonable Faith: Christian Truth and Apologetics,* 3rd ed. Wheaton, IL: Crossway, 2008. Craig explores major arguments for the existence of God at a deeper level.

Dembski, William A. *Intelligent Design: The Bridge Between Science & Theology.* Downers Grove, IL: InterVarsity Press, 2002. You've heard the term, "Intelligent Design"? Here's the seminal work on the subject. It's a hard read, but worth knowing the actual arguments.

Geivett, R. Douglas, and Gary R. Habermas, eds. *In Defense of Miracles: A Comprehensive Case for God's Action in History.* Downers Grove, IL: InterVarsity Press, 1997. Geivett and Habermas build a strong case for the existence of miracles as part of God's working in the world; academic text.

Habermas, Gary R. *The Risen Jesus and Future Hope.* Lanham, MD: Rowman and Littlefield, 2003. Habermas offers an in-depth defense of the historicity of the resurrection of Jesus.

Hummel, Charles E. *The Galileo Connection: Resolving Conflicts Between Science & the Bible.* Downers Grove, IL: InterVarsity Press, 1986. Hummel touches on origins of the universe theories, old earth/young earth controversies, the creation-science controversy, and sets straight the controversy between Galileo and the church.

Moreland, J. P. *Christianity and the Nature of Science: A Philosophical Investigation.* 2nd ed. Grand Rapids: Baker, 1999. This book argues that science and faith are not at odds; it investigates the limits of science.

_____. *Scaling the Secular City: A Defense of Christianity.* Grand Rapids: Baker, 1987. This book is Moreland's seminal work at an academic level. Moreland is one of the top Christian philosophers.

Schaeffer, Francis A. *How Shall We Then Live? The Rise and Decline of Western Thought and Culture.* Grand Rapids: Revell, 1976. Schaeffer's classic work, this book demonstrates how culture influences our lives and faith, what influences culture, and what we should do about it.

LIST OF BOOKS IN ACCORDANCE WITH SURVEY QUESTIONS

1. Does science make faith obsolete?

Dembski, William A. *Intelligent Design: The Bridge Between Science and Theology.* Downers Grove, IL: InterVarsity Press, 2002.

_____. and Michael R. Licona, eds. *Evidence for God: 50 Arguments for Faith from the Bible, History, Philosophy, and Science.* Grand Rapids: Baker, 2010.

Geisler, Norman L., and Frank Turek. *I Don't Have Enough Faith to Be an Atheist.* Wheaton, IL: Crossway, 2004.

Hummel, Charles E. *The Galileo Connection: Resolving Conflicts Between Science & the Bible.* Downers Grove, IL: InterVarsity Press, 1986.

McGrath, Alister, and Joanna Collicutt McGrath. *The Dawkins Delusion?: Atheist Fundamentalism and the Denial of the Divine.* Downers Grove, IL: InterVarsity Press, 2010.

Moreland, J. P. *Christianity and the Nature of Science: A Philosophical Investigation.* Grand Rapids: Baker, 1999.

_____. *Scaling the Secular City: A Defense of Christianity.* Grand Rapids: Baker, 1987.

Strobel, Lee. *The Case for a Creator: A Journalist's Personal Investigation of the Evidence for Jesus.* Grand Rapids: Zondervan, 1998.

2. Is there evidence of the resurrection?

Geivett, R. Douglas and Gary R. Habermas, eds. *In Defense of Miracles: A Comprehensive Case for God's Action in History.* Downers Grove, IL: InterVarsity Press, 1997.

Habermas, Gary R. *The Risen Jesus and Future Hope.* Lanham, MD: Rowman and Littlefield, 2003.

──────. and Michael R. Licona. *The Case for the Resurrection of Jesus.* Grand Rapids: Kregel Publications, 2004.

Strobel, Lee. *The Case for Easter: A Journalist Investigates the Evidence for the Resurrection.* Grand Rapids: Zondervan, 2004.

Turek, Frank and Norman Geisler, *I Don't Have Enough Faith to be an Atheist.* Wheaton, IL: Crossway Books, 2004.

3. Are the Gospels historically reliable?

Evans, Craig A. *Fabricating Jesus: How Modern Scholars Distort the Gospels.* Downers Grove, IL: InterVarsity Press, 2008.

Geisler, Norman L., and Frank Turek. *I Don't Have Enough Faith to Be an Atheist*. Wheaton, IL: Crossway, 2004.
Komoszewski, J. Ed, M. James Sawyer, and Daniel B. Wallace. *Reinventing Jesus: How Contemporary Skeptics Miss the Real Jesus and Mislead Popular Culture*. Grand Rapid: Kregel, 2006.

4) How do I defend my faith to others?

Beckwith, Francis J., and Gregory Koukl. *Relativism: Feet Firmly Planted in Mid-Air*. Grand Rapids: Baker, 1998.
Keller, Timothy. *The Reason for God: Belief in an Age of Skepticism*. New York: Riverhead, 2009.
Koukl, Gregory. *Tactics: A Game Plan for Discussing Your Christian Convictions*. Grand Rapids: Zondervan, 2009.
Sire, James W. *The Universe Next Door: A Basic Worldview Catalog*. 4th ed. Downers Grove, IL: InterVarsity Press, 2009.

5. How can I have an open dialog with an atheist?

Keller, Timothy. *The Reason for God: Belief in an Age of Skepticism*. New York: Riverhead, 2009.
Koukl, Gregory. *Tactics: A Game Plan for Discussing Your Christian Convictions*. Grand Rapids: Zondervan, 2009.
Newman, Randy. *Questioning Evangelism: Engaging People's Hearts the Way Jesus Did*. Grand Rapids: Kregel, 2004.

6. Is life absurd without God?

Budziszewski, J. *What We Can't Not Know*. San Francisco: Ignatius Press, 2011.
Craig, William Lane. *Reasonable Faith: Christian Truth and Apologetics*. Wheaton, IL: Crossway, 2008.
Schaeffer, Francis A. *How Shall We Then Live? The Rise and Decline of Western Thought and Culture*. Grand Rapids: Revell, 1976.
Zacharias, Ravi. *Can Man Live Without God*. Nashville: Thomas Nelson, 2004.

7. Can you give me a brief introduction to apologetics?

Del Rosario, Mikel. *The Accessible Apologetics Workbook: Five Lessons for Everyday Defenders of the Faith*. Roseville, CA: Apologetics Guy, 2011.

Geisler, Norman L., and Frank Turek. *I Don't Have Enough Faith to Be an Atheist*. Wheaton, IL: Crossway, 2004.

Keller, Timothy. *The Reason for God: Belief in an Age of Skepticism*. New York: Riverhead, 2009.

Powell, Doug. *Holman QuickSource Guide to Christian Apologetics*. Nashville: Broadman & Holman, 2006.

Sharp, Mary Jo. *Why Do You Believe That? A Faith Conversation*, Nashville, TN: LifeWay Press, 2012.

Strobel, Lee. *The Case for Christ: A Journalist's Personal Investigation of the Evidence for Jesus*. Grand Rapids: Zondervan, 1998.

8. What is "faith"?

Lewis, C. S. *Mere Christianity*. San Francisco: HarperCollins, 2001.

Machen, J. Gresham. *What Is Faith?* Carlisle, PA: Banner of Truth, 1996.

Moreland, J. P. and Klaus Issler. *In Search of a Confident Faith: Overcoming Barriers to Trusting in God*. Downers Grove, IL: InterVarsity Press, 2008.

9. How can I learn to critically analyze arguments for and against God?

"Apologetics VII: Critical Thinking." *The Theology Program*. Reclaiming the Mind Ministries [compact disc format]. Available from http://www.reclaimingthemind.org.

Bluedorn, Nathaniel, and Hans Bluedorn. *The Fallacy Detective: Thirty-Eight Lessons on How to Recognize Bad Reasoning*. Portland, OR: Christian Logic, 2009.

Sproul, R. C. *Defending Your Faith: An Introduction to Apologetics*. Wheaton, IL: Crossway, 2009.

10. How can God be good when there is evil in the world?

Copan, Paul. *How Do You Know You're Not Wrong?: Responding to Objections That Leave Christians Speechless*. Grand Rapids: Baker, 2005.
———. *"That's Just Your Interpretation": Responding to Skeptics who Challenge Your Faith*. Grand Rapids: Baker, 2001.
———. *True for You, But Not for Me: Deflating the Slogans That Leave Christians Speechless*. Grand Rapids: Bethany House, 1998.

11. Why Jesus when there are so many other beliefs?

Copan, Paul. *How Do You Know You're Not Wrong?: Responding to Objections that Leave Christians Speechless*. Grand Rapids: Baker, 2005.
———. *"That's Just Your Interpretation": Responding to Skeptics who Challenge Your Faith*. Grand Rapids: Baker, 2001.
———. *True for You, But Not for Me: Deflating the Slogans That Leave Christians Speechless*. Grand Rapids: Bethany House, 1998.
Samples, Kenneth Richard. *A World of Difference: Putting Christian Truth Claims to the Worldview Test*. Grand Rapids: Baker, 2007.
Sire, James W. *The Universe Next Door: A Basic Worldview Catalog*. Downers Grove, IL: InterVarsity Press, 2004.

TRUSTED APOLOGETICS WEB SITES:

www.4truth.net—The apologetics website of the North American Mission Board
www.carm.org—Christian Apologetics & Research Ministry
www.confidentchristianity.com—Confident Christianity (that's me!)
www.reclaimingthemind.org—Reclaiming the Mind Apologetics Ministry

www.bethinking.org—Be Thinking Apologetics (articles specified
by learning level: beginner, intermediate, advanced)
www.str.org—Stand to Reason
www.selflessdefense.com—Selfless Defense Apologetics Ministry
www.answering-islam.org—The largest and most in-depth Christian Web site on Islam
www.apologetics315.com—The most comprehensive collection of
apologetics resources on the web
www.veritas.org—The Veritas Forum

TRUSTED APOLOGISTS' WEB SITES:

www.leestrobel.com—Author Lee Strobel's Web site
www.confidentchristianity.com—Confident Christianity (my Web
site)
www.paulcopan.com—Dr. Paul Copan
www.garyhabermas.com—Dr. Gary Habermas
www.reasonablefaith.org—Dr. William Lane Craig
www.comereason.org—Lenny Esposito
www.normangeisler.com—Dr. Norman Geisler
www.risenjesus.com—Dr. Michael Licona
www.dwillard.org—Dr. Dallas Willard